The *Gifts* of Christmas

A TREASURY OF TRUE STORIES

BARBARA RUSSELL CHESSER

Trilogy Christian Publishers
A Wholly Owned Subsidiary of Trinity Broadcasting Network
2442 Michelle Drive
Tustin, CA 92780

Cover design by: Cornerstone Creative Solutions
Illustrations: Yozart

For information, address Trilogy Christian Publishing
Rights Department, 2442 Michelle Drive, Tustin, Ca 92780.
Trilogy Christian Publishing/ TBN and colophon are trademarks of Trinity Broadcasting Network.

For information about special discounts for bulk purchases, please contact Trilogy Christian Publishing.

Manufactured in the United States of America

10 9 8 7 6 5 4 3 2 1

Library of Congress Cataloging-in-Publication Data is available.

ISBN 978-1-63769-128-1 (Print Book)
ISBN 978-1-63769-129-8 (ebook)

Dedication

In memory of my grandmother
who showed us all how to love others and
celebrate Christmas every day of the year.

Acknowledgments

To Del Chesser, my husband:

> for invaluable input and advice,
> for editing expertise and thoughtful diplomacy,
> for prayer and unending encouragement,
> for a treasured marriage of fifty-five-plus years.

To Kelley Smith Higgs:

> for a friendship that has endured in spite of generational differences and working together to meet deadlines;
> for a magnanimous combination of expertise—writing, editing, organization, and work ethic;
> for mastery of all things spiritual, especially practical application.

Contents

Foreword

The short stories in *The Gifts of Christmas* are such a delight! Based on diverse experiences and rich in personalities, the memorable stories set the stage for a joyful, meaningful Christmas season.

I started to list my favorite stories in this book, but my list quickly grew too long to include in a "Foreword." Several provide laughter, others bring nostalgia for my own childhood, and others are compelling accounts of people grieving through the holidays and finding hope. Some are unusual—and unusually good—and others simply remind us of the real reason for the season.

While I could tell you what I love about every story in *The Gifts of Christmas*, I suggest you read this collection of stories for yourself. Also, give a copy to family members and friends. They will love it, and they will love you for giving it to them.

By the way, I have known Barbara Russell Chesser, PhD, for decades, and she is uniquely qualified to present this collection of stories about people and their Christmas experiences. She has written numerous other award-winning books and countless articles about people. She has even written for *Reader's Digest* and co-authored one of the bestselling Chicken Soup for the Soul books!

Lea N. Taylor,
Lt. Col. (Retired) of the US Army

Preface

Christmas is a time of enjoying family, feasting together on good food, and making memories we will cherish for a lifetime. I invite you to curl up by the fireplace, on the beach, or wherever you are, and let's go down memory lane together. You may be reminded of some of your own Christmas memories when you read the real-life stories I've written for this book:

- When I first met Gertie, she was in jail for stealing food to feed her hungry children. I invite you to read and learn what happened to Gertie.
- My "perfect Christmas" was nothing like what I had planned. Have your plans ever been totally turned upside down?
- Sam, the rich kid in our neighborhood, liked our makeshift toys better than his. His recollection as an adult was surprising.
- When I first set eyes on the best ugliest green bike I'd ever seen, it was love at first sight! What happened next, however, was even better and gave me a memory that has lasted a lifetime.
- The story of four heroic chaplains is one of my favorite stories about courage and sacrifice. Perhaps it will become yours, too.

While I was growing up, my large extended family loved sharing all the nostalgia that was stored away in our memories and our hearts. When I told my daughter, Christi, I wished I had recorded stories told (or "lived out") by my grandmother, mother, two brothers, other family members, and friends, she said, "Why don't you write about some of their stories and also yours?" This book is the result of my saying "Yes" to my daughter. I am grateful Christi encouraged me to share these stories that embrace the gifts of Christmas—love, joy, hope, peace, and faith. I invite you to read them to put you in the mood for a

Merry Christmas!

PART ONE

CELEBRATING THE GIFTS
OF LOVE AND JOY

My Perfect Christmas

Thanks be to God for his indescribable gift!

2 Corinthians 9:15 (NIV)

Triumphantly I tied the string on the last package to be mailed. Shopping had always been difficult. I had a hard time knowing what to buy for the men on my list, and I found women to be fairly picky. This year, though, I felt like I'd chosen the perfect gifts.

My niece was the most difficult to buy for because she was in college, and I did not want to be thought of as an old fuddy-duddy. Each year I tried to get something special to prove I hadn't lost touch completely. This year, because my niece seemed to live from party to party, why not *give* her a party? I bought party hats, plates and napkins, invitations, a board game, and all the other things she would need to throw a nice bash. I made a habit of writing a short note with each gift. For the party, I wrote, "Darling, *love* life and share it with your friends on New Year's Eve."

Next was Aunt Hattie, my elderly aunt who seemed frail and delicate these days. She was the type who opened lilac sachets and lace handkerchiefs for Christmas. I decided to give her a cameo that was an engagement present from my father to my mother many years ago. My mother had given it to me, but I didn't wear it. I knew Aunt Hattie would wear it with joy. I placed it in a box with a note that said, "I received this from the greatest lady I have known and pass it onto the next great lady of our family. Wear it with love."

Next on my list was my pastor. I liked my pastor and wanted to get him something special for Christmas. A recently released book, *Jesus and Alcohol,* fit the bill because he mentioned almost every Sunday the perils of overindulgence. I figured this book might provide a fresh illustration or two. I carefully wrote, "Your words and actions influence so many lives. Thank you for all the good you do."

I'm not sure my pastor would have approved of the gift I bought for my brother. Ever since my brother had married "that woman with all those children," he seemed to need some relief. Perhaps a bottle of fine wine would provide the escape he needed from time to time. On his note, I wrote, "Hope this provides a little sanctuary from all the stress you must be experiencing. Drink it slowly."

Next was my boss. I had worked for him for several years and always respected and admired him, but he never even called me by my first name. He didn't seem to have much of a personal life, much less socializing with people from the office. Because he was a good boss and provided a good living for me, I wanted to get him a thoughtful gift. Not wanting to be too pushy, I ended up buying him a gift certificate from a department store. Thirty-five dollars was a nice gift without looking too eager to please. In my note to him, I simply wrote, "Merry Christmas."

The last gift was for my five-year-old nephew. I selected a cute little teddy bear and wrote a sweet note. I considered my list again and felt I'd selected the right gift for everyone. Packages were wrapped and ready to mail. When I was about to attach the address labels, the phone rang. After I had talked a long time with my friend, I would need to hurry to get to the post office before they closed. I sat down at the table, hurriedly stuck the labels on the packages, and raced off to the post office just in the nick of time.

A few days later, my perfect Christmas began to unravel. Aunt Hattie called in the middle of the day, which was my first clue that something was amiss. She typically called in the evenings. Aunt Hattie sounded frantic. "Barbara, you have to help me!" I asked her what was wrong. She replied, "It is the party! I have never had a party in my whole life. I don't know how, but I do want to have one. And I want to do it right."

It began to make sense. I had mixed up the labels, and Aunt Hattie received the party package I'd intended for my niece. It was too late to straighten things out. Aunt Hattie had used all the invitations and wanted a few more. I realized I had misjudged this frail old lady. Under that ancient exterior burned a heart of youth with a passion for life. I told Aunt Hattie, "We'll throw the best New Year's bash you ever imagined!"

I wondered who had received the cameo. It wasn't the minister because he was opening a bottle of wine and probably asking himself, "What is Barbara trying to tell me? Maybe I have been too harsh about drinking, dancing, and all those things some 'good' Christians deem the worst sins."

Many people commented on how unusual it was to send a five-year-old a gift certificate to a department store. His mother, however, said the gift taught her son a valuable lesson. She spent hours with him as he chose gifts for himself and others. His mother wrote me a note that said, "Your gift helped him experience the joy of giving. He is beginning to understand the real meaning of Christmas."

My brother got the book *Jesus and Alcohol*. He, too, sent a card of thanks. "I hadn't realized my drinking had become so obvious that the family noticed. Thank you for caring enough to be truthful with me. I've read the book and plan to join AA after Christmas."

My niece opened her gift while standing in front of the mirror. The red satin party dress with plunging neckline could not have clashed more with the beautiful cameo. She read the card: "To the next great lady of our family." If she spent the holidays the way she had planned instead of with her family, who would consider her a great lady? With the cameo in one hand, she took the phone in the other hand and called home, "Is it too late to come home, Mom?" That trip home began to heal the relationship between my niece and her mother. I saw the cameo years later on my niece's beautiful wedding gown.

The teddy bear—unless lost in the mail—had gone to my boss. I rehearsed in my mind what to say when I heard from him. I decided to just tell him about the mix-up and get another gift certificate. I brewed a cup of tea and sat down in front of the fire to consider the strange turn of events: Aunt Hattie's party, the pastor's wine (heaven forbid!), the five-year-old's windfall, my brother's new start in life, my niece's cameo, and the teddy bear. Then I remembered the note with the teddy bear! I had written for my young nephew, "My dearest, I wish I could hug as tightly as you will hug this bear. Come to see me, and we'll have a Christmas you'll never forget."

There was no way I could face my boss now. I would have to email or text my resignation! As the tears flowed down my face, the phone rang. It was my boss. He said, "Barbara?"

I gulped and forced out a weak "Yes."

With the cracking voice of a teenage boy, he asked, "What time do you plan Christmas dinner?"

It was a Christmas we all would remember. It did not happen as I had intended, but it was better than I could have ever planned.

That first Christmas in Bethlehem was something like this. God's Messiah was expected. Many thought He would come in glory, overthrowing the Romans and dealing out God's justice and punishment with a stern hand. Only God knew He had to come as an ordinary man, carpenter, teacher, miraculous healer, and friend to the friendless.

Thanks be to God for a perfect first Christmas! And thanks be to God for *my* perfect Christmas![1]

Packing Parachutes and Praying

Coming in on a wing and a prayer...

(A phrase from the prayer of a World War II crew that their bullet-riddled warplane would somehow make it safely back to their base)

"Tell us more!" I pleaded with my mother as I snuggled closer to her. My two older brothers, my mother, and I were wrapped together in warm quilts near our Christmas tree as she told us stories—our favorite pastime! Although we loved hearing stories over and over, she began one we had never heard, "I needed a job..."

Barely twenty-four when my father was accidentally killed at the beginning of World War II, my mother had three young children to care for. She rarely complained, but I do remember her saying when I was older, "Times were tough back then." Fortunately, she found a job at the Air Force base near our home in New Mexico. Soon she was packing parachutes for our brave men to use in World War II.

"I prayed over every parachute I packed," Mother said. Her gentle smile turned more serious as she looked at each one of us and almost whispered, "I also prayed for the one whose life would depend on that parachute being packed perfectly."

My older brother quipped, "But you didn't even know whose parachute it was going to be."

Our mother wisely explained, "No, I didn't know—but God knew."

"Besides," Mother continued, "each prayer was a gift…"

My younger brother interrupted her, "How could they ever give you a gift?"

Mother quickly replied, "I could never repay them or match their gift. They were willing to give their lives." After a pause, our mother took a deep breath and continued, "It was getting close to Christmas when I first started praying for those young men. Miraculously I soon felt less sad and overwhelmed by your father's death, even during the holidays."

That Christmas more than seventy-five years ago is one of my favorite Christmas memories. I do not recall what was inside the boxes wrapped in glitzy paper and tied with colorful ribbons. Rather, I vividly remember being together—sharing, laughing, and loving. Just as the old quilts kept us cozy and snug, this well-worn memory of my mother telling us about her packing parachutes and praying still warms my heart.

Brando's Last Christmas

God would be pleased, I believe, that one of his most special animals—the "dog"—is God spelled backward.

"I always had a dog growing up, and I loved my dogs," Michael, my son-in-law, said. He and my daughter, Christi, had recently returned to the United States from Korea where Michael was stationed, and they had acquired an Italian mastiff. He continued, "When I was in college and early in my military assignments, I couldn't have a dog. So, Christi and I were both eager to get a dog when we could. Many cold evenings in Korea, I spent researching the right kind of dog to get." Michael was trying to convince me it was a good decision in spite of their having a baby—Jackson, my first grandchild. Michael pointed out how Brando at maturity would weigh approximately 110 pounds and be about twenty-eight inches tall.

Michael's research findings did not exactly reassure me. After hearing how large Brando would ultimately be, I was filled with fear. Stories of dogs hurting babies flooded my mind. Michael explained that this breed was characteristically reserved, quiet, stable, even-tempered, trainable, and calm. He added that because of these traits, this breed was used for personal protection, law enforcement, as a guard dog, and as a companion. Michael's final appeal was, "It's the perfect dog for a family with a baby!"

Months went by, and I was greatly relieved that Brando and my grandson were co-surviving. My husband and I were excited to be traveling to Christi's to help celebrate Jackson's first birthday. The day after arriving, Del and I happily accepted the responsibility of caring for Jackson while both parents worked. All went well until mid-afternoon. I was holding Jackson when Brando nuzzled close to Jackson's face as he had numerous times the evening before when Michael or Christi was holding him. Suddenly Brando broke the peace and quiet with a menacing guttural growl and a frightening showing of teeth. Tragedy flashed through my mind. My worst fears were about to come true! But almost as quickly as Brando went into attack mode, he closed his mouth and turned away in silence. Shaken, Del and I put Brando in the fenced-in backyard.

When Michael arrived home, we explained what happened. "No wonder," Michael said laughingly as he brought Brando out of his captivity. Holding up Brando's ear, Michael pointed at the teeth marks in his soft, velvety ear. "It took a lot of restraint on Brando's part not to retaliate," Michael said. Jackson obviously had used his new, sharp teeth to "dig into" Brando's ear.

A year or so later, Michael was scheduled to work in military airport security in Atlanta. Christi asked me to come to stay with her and Jackson during Michael's absence. Only months since the September 11, 2001 attacks on the World Trade Center and the Pentagon, emotions were still raw. So, of course, I was on the first plane there. One evening someone knocked loudly at the front door. Before Christi could get the door fully open, a disheveled, scary-looking man was rattling the storm door and demanding that he come in out of the cold to deliver the food we had ordered and to get paid for it. "I have not ordered any food," my daughter insisted. The shifty man became angry and clanged the door even more vigorously. Terrified, I almost stopped breathing as I thought, *What do we do next?*

Brando was taking his evening nap, but when awakened by the noise, he sprang into action. In one gigantic leap, Brando was at the front door. By now, he was a large dog, and his growl was even larger. He dropped his jaw, revealing a terrifying arsenal of large, sharp teeth, and let out a hair-raising growl. The "deliveryman" dropped his grip on the storm door. One more ghastly growl from Brando and the sketchy fellow stumbled all over himself to get to his car and disappear into the darkness of the night.

By the time Brando was fully grown, he, along with the rest of the family, moved to New Orleans, Michael's new duty station. Housing on the base was vintage; like the other rooms, the living room was tiny. Now a full-fledged family member, Brando was lovingly welcomed to join the rest of his family in the living room. He was given the best seat in the house, right in the middle of the room. Ava, the youngest addition to the family, let him get comfortable first, and then she snuggled close to him like he was her warm, cuddly bean bag. He peacefully enjoyed Ava's company. That is, until she put her tiny fingers up his nostrils. He would shake his head to dislodge her fingers. When Ava persisted, he turned his head toward her and affectionately swiped his tongue—almost as long as his body—across her face.

Brando continued to work his way into the hearts of every family member, including Del, my husband. A daily walk around the base was a favorite daily ritual of both when we were visiting. Brando considered the base his exclusive domain, and he determined their route, the pace, and when and where to take rest stops. His coat was of an impressive bronze color, and he was strongly built, elegant, and distinguished. His large head and expressive amber eyes were his most dominant features. Brando also earned the friendship of others who lived on the base, including one high-ranking officer who said Brando's size and demeanor commanded respect. This officer always addressed him as "Brando, Sir" (emphasis on "Sir").

"No time to talk. We're locking up our house and leaving now!" My daughter's call was good news. Katrina, a major hurricane, was gaining strength and headed directly to New Orleans. I was relieved that Christi and her family were evacuating along with more than a million other New Orleans and Gulf Coast residents. Little did I know that other dangers would be lurking along the way to safety.

Parked at the edge of a gas station overcrowded by others fleeing from Katrina, Christi had finished filling her car with gas. She was waiting for Michael to buy some snacks and return to his nearby vehicle so they could resume their trip to safety. A loud rap on the car's window startled Christi. Two men glared at her. One of them leaned even closer to the glass and snarled, "Open your window!" He began rubbing his thumb and fingers together, indicating, "Give me money." Before Christi could respond, Brando lurched from his sleeping position in the back seat, pounded on the window with his huge paws, barked and growled furiously, and curled his lips back to show the two men his sharp teeth. As both men abruptly turned and ran into the gridlock of other cars, Christi said to her faithful guardian, "Good job, Brando!"

One Christmas, Del and I were visiting Christi and her family, and we were enjoying all the holiday traditions together. There was a Christmas tree, holiday lights, and stockings for all the family, including Brando. One morning after a brisk morning walk, Brando was drinking from his water dish and splashed water on the floor for the third time that day. As I got down on my knees to mop up the water, I asked him, "Brando, do you think you are worth all this trouble?" Flashbacks instantly filled my mind with the good times this lovable dog had given us. "I'll forgive you for splashing a little water. If I had to drink water out of a dish on the floor, I'd probably splash it everywhere too." After a pause, I added, "I hope you will forgive me for being critical." Immediately Brando's face lighted up and turned into a heart-touching expression that only dogs can make. And I am quite certain he smiled as his warm amber eyes looked straight into my eyes. His entire countenance clearly said, "Of course, I forgive you."

Before the next Christmas, Brando was diagnosed with cancer, and his remarkable life sadly came to an end. I could not believe the pain that hit my heart and each family member's heart. I cherish that last Christmas with Brando, and I am so thankful I made room for him—in my heart and in my life. Loving an animal that I feared and denounced so much at first but later sharing in the love and devotion he gave so fully and richly deepened my understanding of Christmas, the season of love—and forgiveness.

A Hand to Hold

Yet I am always with you; you hold
me by my right hand.

Psalm 73:23 (NIV)

As Dave and Bethany drove along a narrow country road, the old, deserted farmhouse finally came into view.

"Well, this is it," Dave said. "Let's go in."

With obvious annoyance, Bethany answered, "You go. I'll wait."

"Come on," he urged. "I'll show you where I used to watch for old Santa."

Impatiently, Bethany snapped, "Go ahead and get it over with."

Bethany watched as Dave waded through the knee-high grass to the old house, alone. Dave was exploring his past, but Bethany seethed in the present. They were on their way home from a month-long argument, and this trip had been a sort of last-ditch effort to save a crumbling marriage. Always a go-getter, Dave was working long and hard to reach his career goals while Bethany was feeling increasingly left out, neglected, yearning for attention, and a sense of being needed.

"Come on," Dave called from a broken window. "I just saw Grandpa's ghost come down the stairs. No telling who you might see here." He was trying hard to be light-hearted. Bethany wasn't amused.

When Dave finally came back to the car, he was carrying a No Trespassing sign that had fallen down in the grass. "You're not going to take that thing home, I hope," Bethany said. He didn't answer. Taking a marker, he printed something on the sign. Then he went back, set it up in front of the old house, and disappeared inside. The sign now read, "Little Davey Slept Here."

This piqued Bethany's interest enough for her to get out of the car and make her way through the tall grass. When she entered the house, Dave was standing in the middle of the room, amid dust and cobwebs and bits of broken plaster fallen from the ceiling. This was the parlor that was used as a bedroom when company came, he explained. A bed had stood in the corner, with a headboard as high as his grandfather.

Bethany followed Dave to the kitchen, where he showed her where the old cookstove used to stand and the wood box he had filled so many times for Grandma. After a wistful silence, he pointed out where the Christmas stockings would have hung near the fireplace.

Upstairs was a big, forlorn-looking room with one tall window. "I used to lie on the bed here and imagine that window reached right up to the sky."

Bethany softened at the nostalgia she could see in Dave's eyes as he looked around the room. "I understand now why you wanted to come back here," she said. "It was home to you, wasn't it?"

"No. Not home. Just a here-today-gone-tomorrow sort of place. As a feisty little boy with no parents, I was too much for my grandparents. I'd be here a few weeks; then an aunt or uncle would take me to their house for a while until they passed me off to other relatives. Wherever I happened to be, my suitcase was always under the bed, waiting to go when they grew tired of me."

Dave described a particular time he remembered visiting his cousins. "A row of clothing hooks hung on the wall, just our height. Each one had a name under it, and no one dared to use another's hook. It was the same during the holidays: stockings hung by the chimney, each bearing the name of one of my cousins. Gee, I thought, if I only had my own stocking or a hook like my cousins had! I finally found one and asked Aunt Millie, 'Could I please put my name on that empty one?' 'Oh, you won't need it,' she told me. 'You won't even be here next week.' I ran out on the porch and cried my heart out."

Dave continued, "I will never forget the time my cousin Curt hurt himself. Aunt Millie gathered him up in her lap to bandage his toe and held him for a while to stop his crying. I remember standing by the screen door watching; it seemed to me the most wonderful thing in the world to have a mother hold your hand and then hold you close while she bandaged your toe and say, 'Never mind, Dear. Everything's going to be all right.'"

That's what Dave had wanted his whole life. He pondered, "Just someone to hold my hand when I was hurt or lonely; a place to live that was *my* home, this week and next week and always; and my own hook to hang my coat on, my own stocking with my name on it."

Dave sat on the dusty windowsill and pulled Bethany close beside him. He tried to be casual as he related his story, but the vivid picture tore at his emotions.

Seeing her husband as a lonely, motherless six-year-old in this very room opened a new part of Bethany's heart. She could imagine his hearing the winter winds rattling the windows of that old farmhouse, peering out through the frosted panes. The moon seemed to be his only comfort, giving the lonely little fellow the only light in the dark, shivery room.

Dave recounted the night long ago when he had overheard Grandpa saying to Aunt Alice, "We'll bring the boy over in the morning. He's big enough to fetch the wood for you. I'll come for that calf next week." So, he'd been traded off, Dave assumed, for a calf. He'd never again get to sit for hours in Grandpa's beautiful black buggy and pretend he was driving a team of prancing black horses. The buggy would still have its own special place in the barn. *It* had a home. Only little boys were traded like calves. The six-year-old crawled out of bed, his small body shivering. As he looked out the window, he pleaded, "Please, Mr. Man in the Moon, don't let Grandpa trade me off. *Please* let me stay."

"I bawled myself to sleep that night," Dave said, chuckling as if it were funny. Bethany realized that her husband's hand had somehow stolen into hers, and she was grasping it tightly. But it was not just the hand of her husband that she was holding so protectively; it was also the hand of a very small, very frightened, heartbroken little boy. At that moment, Bethany knew they both needed each other.

As the two drove down that country road away from the old house, Dave and Bethany turned a corner in their marriage. In the following years, a nearness and dearness grew between them. Bethany would forever see the reflection of the little fellow who only wanted a hook to hang his clothes on, a Christmas stocking with his name stitched on it, a place to call home, and someone to hold his hand when he was hurt. "Never mind, dear. Everything's going to be all right."

As the days turned into years, Dave and Bethany had a renewed sense of needing one another and being there for one another. Life and marriage continued to bring challenges, of course. But the response remained the same—a tightening of his hand on hers.

One day years later, Dave and Bethany were preparing for Christmas in their home. They were trimming the tree and hanging stockings when Dave had sudden and severe chest pains. Bethany rode close beside Dave in the ambulance and held his hand on the way to the hospital.

Later, Bethany described the brief moment when their eyes met. "Was it a split second of awareness? I will never know for certain. But my heart tells me that the little hurting six-year-old boy heard and understood my message, for I felt a tightening of his hand as I said one last time, 'Never mind, Dear. Everything's going to be all right.'"

The next Christmas, Bethany would decorate her tree and hang the stockings alone, but she found comfort in the memory of their last moments together. And when she found the stocking with Dave's name on it, she knew he'd found a home with her and that he had always had a hand to hold.[2]

The Best Ugliest Green Bike Ever

Beauty is in the eye of the beholder.

Margaret Wolfe Hungerford

It was love at first sight! It was the most beautiful bike I had ever seen. I was seven years old and had gone with my mother to find an employee for my grandmother's café. We had trouble locating the prospective worker's house because street signs were almost non-existent in the part of town where we were searching.

Finally, we saw a crowd gathered around a house. Mother looked for a place to park in the helter-skelter arrangement of old, mostly worn-out cars. "Maybe someone here will know where this address is," Mother mumbled mostly to herself.

Just then, Mother recognized the person she was looking for. This lady had come into the café several weeks ago and told the employee at the cash register she was desperate for a job. The employee took her name and address but no phone number. When she said, "I don't have a phone," her young daughter, who had said nothing until then, blurted out, "'Cause we can't afford one."

As we got closer to the house, we could see that it was a garage sale that had attracted the crowd. Mother was headed toward the woman in charge while I headed straight for the items on the tables.

Then I saw it. I wanted that bike more than anything I had ever thought I wanted! The most wonderful characteristic of the bike was that it was a girl's bike. I had never ridden a girl's bike before. The only bike I had ever ridden belonged to Sam, the seven-year-old considered to be the rich kid in our neighborhood. His bike was better than any of the bikes owned by the other five boys in our neighborhood. Sam was the only one who let me ride his bike, and that was not very often because my two older brothers always wanted to ride it too. I only got to have a turn when Sam or my brothers weren't riding.

As I stared at the green bike for sale, it became more beautiful by the minute. If it were my bike, none of the boys in the neighborhood would want to ride it. Only a sissy would ride a girl's bike.

Another consideration: bikes were stolen from our neighborhood. Some suspected the teenager considered the meanest one in our area. They figured he took the stolen bikes to another part of town and sold them there. The way I looked at it was the green bike at this garage sale was so ugly no one would steal it because they probably knew no one would buy it. So, the longer I gazed at this ugly green bike, the more beautiful it became.

To keep someone else from buying the bike, I pushed it to where my mother was talking to the prospective employee. Not concerned about good manners, I immediately interrupted my mother, "Please, please, buy this bike for me. I love it! You won't need to buy me any other Christmas presents." Seeing that my mother did not appear to be in the buying mode, I added emphatically, "It can also count for my birthday present!" Next came the inevitable question, "How much is it?" When I told my mother, she quickly replied, "We cannot afford it, Honey. I am sorry."

The other mother saw how upset I was. She said, "You can ride it around here while your mother and I talk." Without another word, I jumped on that ugliest green bike I had ever seen and rode it down the driveway and onto the street.

It was the most exhilarating feeling in the world! As I rode back toward my mother, I noticed how they both seemed different. Their voices sounded friendly, and their smiles spoke volumes.

"Put the bike in the car," my mother said. I could hardly believe my ears. Stunned, I stood in silence while I heard the other mother say, "Thank you for the job. I will be there tomorrow." Everybody was happy, especially me.

I have received some splendid presents in my lifetime. At the time, I thought the ugliest green bike ever was the most awesome one. As I grew older, I realized that a far greater gift was given to me. I saw two single moms working together so their kids could have Christmas gifts they would treasure. I learned that to buy the bike, my mother had spent the tip money she had been saving to buy herself a new dress and shoes. This was a big sacrifice because my mother almost never bought anything for herself. The other mother expressed her gratitude for being given a job.

I saw a perfect picture of a mother's love that day. This Christmas memory is a gift that has lasted a lifetime—just thinking about it still makes my heart smile.

A Professional

Lord, teach us to pray.

Luke 11:1 (NIV)

A woman received a phone call that her young daughter was very sick. The worried mother left work immediately, stopped by the pharmacy, and worked her way through the busy Christmas crowd to get some medication. Upon returning to her car, she found she had locked her keys inside.

Not knowing what to do, she frantically called the babysitter. She answered, "You might find a coat hanger and use that to open the door."

The desperate mother shouted to nearby shoppers scurrying to their cars, "Does anyone have a coat hanger?" Miraculously someone rushed over to her with a bent-up hanger and quickly disappeared in the crowded parking lot. Her heart sinking, the mother stared at the hanger and moaned, "I don't know how to use this." She pleaded to God for help.

An old rusty car pulled up, driven by a dirty, greasy man with a scruffy beard and a biker skull rag on his head. The woman cried, "Dear God, this is what you sent to help me?" The man got out of his car and asked if he could be of assistance. "Yes," she gasped and then explained, "My daughter is quite sick. I must get home to her. Please, can you use this hanger to unlock my car?"

Without hesitating, he smiled ever so slightly and replied, "Sure," and walked confidently over to her car. In seconds he had the car door opened.

Relieved, she hugged the man and, through her tears, blurted out, "Thank you so much! You are such a nice man."

"Lady," the man replied, "I ain't a nice man. I just got out of prison." Seeing the woman's frightened reaction, he added, "I am on my way home for Christmas. I was in prison 'cause I stole a car."

The woman hugged the man again and cried out: "Thank you, God, for sending me a professional!"[3]

A Bracelet Revisited

Christmas is most truly Christmas when we celebrate it
by giving the light of love to those who need it most.

Ruth Carter Stapleton

Sights and sounds of Christmas were everywhere in my home-town. But as my grandmother and I bounced along a rough, bone-rattling country road on our way to the home of my once-upon-a-time friend, I was not in a Christmas mood. In contrast, thoughts of anger, confrontation, and revenge swirled like a New Mexico sandstorm in my teenage mind.

The rugged road led us to a small, dilapidated house that looked as if no one lived there: gaping holes in the screen door, paint peeling off the weathered wood, and age-old garbage and junk scattering the yard. As we drove closer, I thought about the treasurer of our ninth-grade club, "No wonder she didn't want me to come here."

Collecting money from the members to buy a gift for our outstanding member was the treasurer's job. A committee chose the gift, but I was in charge of paying for it and getting it to the Christmas party only two days away. When I pressed the treasurer for the money, she simply said, "I'm sorry. I don't have it anymore." I was left "holding the bag," and at my insis-tence, Grandmother had driven me to the treasurer's house to get the money.

After parking and going to the door, we knocked several times before a woman with a fear-wracked expression on her face opened the door. We entered a nearly empty room: no Christmas tree, no lights, no signs of the holiday, or much else for that matter. The starkness shocked me, but my unflappable grandmother calmly thanked the weary woman for inviting us in and asking her warmly, "How are you this evening?"

Taking the question seriously, the woman began spilling out her dreadful circumstances. She had lost her job, her car needed serious repairs, and her husband had fled the desperate situation months ago. Grandmother listened attentively.

By the time we left, Grandmother had assured the distraught mother a job in her café as well as a ride home each evening until she could get her car repaired. As we were saying our goodbyes, Grandmother hugged the mother as if they had known each other forever and then looked at the daughter, smiled, and said, "I am glad you and Barbara are friends."

The doors of our car had barely closed when I indignantly demanded, "What about the money?" While Grandmother drove in complete silence, exasperation screamed inside me. Eventually, she replied, "What about the money?" The tone of her question was different from mine. Too stunned to say anything, I suffered through another wearisome stretch of silence before Grandmother said softly, "I will pay for the bracelet."

By the time my grandmother and I reached the end of the windblown road, a Christmas star and other twinkle lights on the tall grain silo shed a mystical glow on that entire side of town. As we drove on, we saw hints of the holidays all around, and we listened to the sounds of the season as they hummed on the radio.

When we turned into our well-paved street, the Christmas lights were sparkling brighter than ever on the eves of the houses, and the Christmas trees in the windows seemed to glow more beautifully than when we left to "get the money."

My anger was being displaced by a sympathetic understanding of my friend's grim home life. My determination to confront her was melting into compassion, and my quest for revenge was being transformed into forgiveness.

As we walked into our house, Grandmother put her arm around my shoulder, turned, looked deep into my eyes, and said, "Remember, there are always two sides to every story."

My grandmother made sure the bracelet was purchased, but more than that, she made sure I understood the real riches of Christmas...Understanding. Compassion. Forgiveness. Grandmother's words of wisdom have been a lifelong treasure.

Daily Prayer

Then you will call on me and come and
pray to me, and I will listen to you.

Jeremiah 29:12 (NIV)

The Christmas season brings out "the better angels" in people.
A friend of mine, the late John T. Baker, contended that this
desire may be reflected in our prayers. He combined this belief
with his sense of humor when he wrote this prayer:

Dear Lord—
I'm proud to say, so far today
I've got along all right;
I have not gossiped, whined, or bragged,
Or had a single fight.
I haven't lost my temper once,
Or criticized my mate,
I have not lied, I have not cried,
Or loudly cursed my fate.
So far today, I've not one time
Been grumpy or morose,
I've not been spiteful, cold, or vain,
Self-centered or verbose.
But, Lord, I'm going to need your help
Throughout the hours ahead,
So give me strength, Dear Lord, for now
I'm getting out of bed.

Christmas Lilacs from Janet

God moves in mysterious ways.

William Cowper

Although it occurred more than forty years ago, there is one Labor Day weekend I will never forget. My youngest sister, Janet, and her husband, Robert, were riding leisurely back into town from our mother's country home. They had taken their young toddler to our mother to babysit so they could eat out with friends. As they were entering the outskirts of town and only a few blocks from their home, a drunk driver ran a stop sign. In a few seconds of screeching tires, flying glass, and a senseless snarl of steel, the drunk driver ended the lives of the young couple. Their little son would never see his parents again. They would never again experience the joy of playing with him. The three of them would never return to their home.

That first Thanksgiving after this family tragedy came before our family felt any sense of holiday gratitude. Mother's grief over Janet's death was unbearable, and it intensified vivid memories of prior losses. Mother was young when her father died in the 1918 flu epidemic. A baby born to her mother about a year after remarrying died on his first birthday, another emotional trauma for a young girl like my mother. My father was accidentally killed and buried on her twenty-fourth birthday. She was left with three young children, including me, to rear. Ten years later, she married a widower and had a second family of three daughters. Janet was the youngest, and after all the other losses in my mother's life, Janet's death was heart-rending and simply more than Mother could handle.

Christmas was even more agonizing. This yuletide holiday is supposed to be joyous with love, hope, and peace filling the hearts of everyone, and families are supposed to be laughing, sharing happy memories of days gone by, and having a good time. Yet, there was no display of these expectations. In contrast, grief gripped our hearts. Mother's heart was crushed more than ours. Even with God's help, Mother simply could not dig out of the deep pit of despair over Janet's death.

The next year, on the first Labor Day weekend anniversary of Janet and Robert's deaths, several of us gathered at my mother's home in hopes we could help ease her pain, but a dark cloud still hung over our family. When Mother and I were in the family room alone, she picked up a book and opened it to a poem by Alfred Lord Tennyson:

> O Christ, that it were possible
> For one short hour to see
> The souls we loved, that they may tell us
> What and where they be.

After reading the poem, I asked Mother, "You think about Janet a lot, don't you?" She nodded in agreement, wiped tears from her eyes, and said, "No hurt is worse than the death of a child. It takes away your will to live."

After a long silence, Mother looked toward the lilac bushes lining the back lawn and commented, "It seems so strange that the lilac bushes did not bloom this year." After a pause, she continued, "As a young girl, Janet couldn't wait for the buds to burst into beautiful, sweet-smelling blossoms. She would reach up to the blossoms to pat them, and often she stood on her tiptoes to pull a blossom to her nose to smell its sweet aroma." Mother's face turned even sadder as she said, "Just a few days before Janet was killed, she had cut several stems of lilac blossoms and put them in a vase for the dinner table that evening."

As Mother talked, a few other family members came in, sat down, and listened. With sadness reflected in her eyes, she looked at us and told us what we already knew, "Janet's death sucked the life out of me." The flowering lilac bushes must have felt the same way, for, after Janet's death, there were no more colorful blossoms despite the warm New Mexico sun.

Nothing else was said about the lilacs as the conversation turned to other topics in the few days before we returned home.

Every week I called Mother. We chatted about our week's activities, plans for the next week, and other inconsequential trivia before we talked about Janet. Losing her youngest daughter so tragically seemingly overwhelmed her, although she always interjected, "I know God cares." When she cried, I was reminded of some lines from an old song:

> I see God when a mother cries.
> I see God in a love that never dies.

As the months rolled on, the lilac bushes still refused to bloom. My brother told me that Mother said to him, "I know just how they feel." Because Christmas intensified Mother's sadness, I was dreading the approaching holidays.

One early December afternoon, after returning from a three-day trip, Mother called me. "You will not believe it!" she said with an excitement in her voice I had not heard since Janet was killed. "They are beautiful!" she said. Not giving me a chance to ask what she was talking about, she continued, words racing over each other. When she pulled into the driveway, two beautiful clusters of lilac blossoms had exploded into view.

"They were on the first bush," Mother explained, "and they were the largest clusters and the most vibrant color I had ever seen!" In a hushed whisper, Mother said, "My prayers have been answered. Janet loved lilacs, and when two of the most beautiful clusters of them appeared, an amazing peace filled my heart."

Mother continued, "Christmas will be so much happier this year. Those blossoms were a Christmas message from Janet. She wants me to know she's okay. God answers prayers in different ways." With a heartfelt smile, Mother added: "This time, it was the return of the lilacs."

PS: Merry Hanukkah and Happy Christmas

> Blessed is the season which engages the
> whole world in a conspiracy of love.
> *Hamilton Wright Mabie*

My protestant friend, who lost her mate several years ago, recently developed a relationship with a Jewish man who had also lost his spouse. In spite of their different religions, they seemed a perfect match. Fortunately, all their children gave their blessings on the marriage. While they were excited about their upcoming wedding a few days after Hanukkah and a few days before Christmas, they did not need more crystal vases, toasters, or dishes. This was the invitation:

Phil, Richard, Karen, and Allison,
and
David, Samuel, and Sarah
request the honor of your presence
at the marriage of their
Mother and Father.
Because they are combining two households,
they already have at least two of everything.
So please, no presents!
Reception and garage sale immediately
following the ceremony.
PS: Merry Hanukkah and Happy Christmas![4]

My Mother's Christmas List

The best and most beautiful things in the world cannot be
seen or even touched—they must be felt with the heart.

Helen Keller

"This is the worst Christmas of my life," I cried out at my two
brothers as I was stuffing some clothes into my suitcase. The
week before Christmas at my grandmother's café was always
hectic—more work to do than time to do it. Childcare was a
challenge, so our mother had arranged for my Aunt Ruth to
take my two brothers and me home with her and her family
for a few days.

Spending time away from home with cousins was fun
during the summer, but not during the days right before
Christmas. For three kids, ages six, seven, and eight, being at
home with our mother was what we wanted most. After our
father was killed in an accident five years prior, we had been
forced to start a new life, one quite different from when our
father was managing a ranch and our mother was taking care
of us.

In our new routine, we became a close-knit family. While
waiting for our mother to come home from work at the café,
my brothers and I often gathered in the living room of our
tiny three-room house to listen to our favorite programs on the
radio. Upon her arrival home, Mother joined us; her laughter
made the programs even more delightful. At bedtime, we all
piled onto one of the twin beds so she could read stories to

us. (In wintry weather, to combat the shock of the cold sheets, we all cuddled under the covers.) For breakfast, Mother made us hot buttery cinnamon toast. Warm, cozy times with our mother made me want to spend time with her and not with relatives, especially on Christmas Day.

When our aunt picked us up, we were glad to see our cousins and tolerated the drive to their house in the country. On Christmas Eve, the day we were scheduled to go home, the unthinkable happened! All hopes for our being home for Christmas morning were shattered when Aunt Ruth told us a frozen water pipe had burst in the pumphouse, and our trip home was postponed until Christmas Day!

Watching our cousins open their presents was agonizing, but we faced a bigger challenge: my brothers and I had not bought Mother any gifts! Not knowing that we would be sent home with relatives, we had planned on buying her gifts when my aunt took us home before Christmas Day.

After finally getting home, we instantly glued our eyes on the presents under the scrawny Christmas tree. (The decorations were even scrawnier, for we had hurriedly made them before we were whisked away.) As soon as Aunt Ruth and her family left, we did not waste any time opening our presents.

Our exuberance was short-lived when we remembered that we had no gifts for our mother. Curious as to why our mood had suddenly turned so somber, she asked, "Why are you so sad? Don't you like your presents?"

Sobbing, we tried to convince Mother we felt awful because we had no gifts for her. In her loving way, she placed us one by one under the tree. As she nestled each of us near the branches, she said, "Listen closely. You have given me the best presents you can ever imagine." Puzzled, we listened as Mother looked at each of us crouched awkwardly among the branches.

"You three, sitting around this Christmas tree, are at the top of my Christmas wish list. *You* are my gifts!"

My mother's words are a divine reminder that the most precious gifts are not expensive, beautifully wrapped items bought in a store. They are ones felt with the heart.

Gertie's Grit and Gumption—and Gift

Lord, make me an instrument of your peace;
Where there is hatred, let me sow love;
Where there is injury, pardon;
Where there is doubt, faith;
Where there is despair, hope;
Where there is darkness, light;
And where there is sadness, joy.
O Divine Master,
Grant that I may not so much seek
To be consoled as to console;
To be understood, as to understand;
To be loved, as to love;
For it is in giving that we receive,
It is in pardoning that we are pardoned,
And it is in dying that we are born to Eternal Life.
Amen.

St. Francis of Assisi

Incidents flood my memories of seeing St. Francis's prayer in action. One memory stands out, and although it happened decades ago, I will never forget it. I was in high school at the time, and the school had let out for the Christmas holidays.

The county sheriff was eating at my grandmother's café. She was greeting customers and chatting with others when the sheriff motioned to her. She went closer to him to hear what he had to say. He said to her, "Mattie, there's a young woman named Gertie in jail because she stole some food items from a grocery store." He took a deep breath and then whispered hoarsely, "I just found out it was to feed her two young children."

The sheriff captured my grandmother's undivided attention with his last comment. Her eyes opened even wider, and her usual smile turned solemn as she said, "What if I pay her bail and give her a job?" With no hesitation, the sheriff replied, "She's yours." He knew my grandmother meant business. So, he added, "Meet you at the courthouse."

That day, I had come to the café to order a hamburger. I was walking toward the front of the café toward Grandmother when I overheard most of the conversation between the sheriff and her. When she saw me, she told me to put my hamburger in a sack, get her car from the parking area in the back of the café, and meet her at the courthouse. By the time I drove to the courthouse, Grandmother had paid Gertie's bail, and both women were standing at the curb of the Courthouse Square.

Counting the money as she handed it to Gertie, Grandmother said, "You buy groceries for yourself and your little girls." As Grandmother opened the car door for Gertie, she said, "My granddaughter, Barbara, will help you buy groceries and drive you to your house." Before closing the car door, Grandmother added, "She will pick you up tomorrow by nine o'clock. Since it is Saturday, we will really need your help to handle the Christmas crowd. One of my waitresses who lives close to you will pick you up for work next week." I was just about to drive away when Grandmother knocked on Gertie's window and said to her, "You'll make it. You have grit and gumption, and your two little girls need you."

Grandmother gave Gertie a job and made arrangements for her transportation. My grandmother undoubtedly remembered how it felt to be a desperate young mother with young children to feed. She was twenty-four when her husband died in the Spanish flu pandemic. She had three young girls. The oldest was five, and the youngest (my mother) was eleven months old. Grandmother worked in the fields by day and took in laundry at night to be able to feed her three young daughters.

So, off Gertie and I went to the grocery store. I was surprised, and so was Gertie, that the sheriff was there to greet us. He wanted to explain to the manager that the young mother had served her time in jail for stealing groceries from the small store and would be purchasing groceries that day. The store was close to her house, and she did not yet have a car, but she did have a job. As I was leaving Gertie's house after taking her home, she said with a smile and tears in her eyes, "This is my answered prayer."

Grandmother was an instrument of God's peace that day. Where there was despair, she sowed hope, and where there was sadness, she sowed joy. St. Francis also said, "It is in giving that we receive." Watching Grandmother give so generously that day, I realize now that I was also receiving a real gift. To know clearly that God answers prayer is surely one of the greatest gifts of all—at Christmastime and always.

Sam's Perfect Timing

Like golden apples set in silver is a word
spoken at the right time.

Proverbs 25:11 (ISV)

It was New Year's Eve. Festive Christmas decorations still adorned the small hospital conference room. Huddled together, we felt no holiday cheer and certainly did not look forward to a Happy New Year. "This cannot be happening," my heart cried out when an ICU nurse slung open the door and said, "He is dying. Hurry if you want to be with him!"

After a few minutes, my brother Butch was pronounced dead. Penny, his inconsolable widow, and I trudged back to the small room where other family members were waiting. As I sat down, numbness spread throughout my body. I was exhausted from the frantic 350-mile trip, so I could hold his hand for one last time and tell him I loved him. Watching my brother and lifelong friend die was heartbreaking.

We soon left to spend the night in a nearby hotel. I could not sleep, for scenes of my life raced through my mind. My two brothers were my closest friends, and they frequently appeared in those memories. We played together, fought together, stood up for each other, and encouraged one another through some tough family times. Our friendship remained strong even after we had families of our own and as we grew older.

Six months earlier, our older brother, Phill, had been diagnosed with stage four pancreatic cancer. My heart still aching from Phill's dying on that hot July day, I leaned on Butch even more. That Christmas Eve, Phill's birthday, Butch and I enjoyed a long phone conversation about how much Phill meant to us and how much we missed him.

As the dark night finally gave way to a chilly, cloudy day, my husband and I went to meet the family for breakfast. In hushed voices, the family began planning what to do next. "Relatives must be notified," my take-charge husband said. Because it was early morning, we agreed on no phone calls, just emails. When I opened my cell phone to begin sending emails, I was stunned. A long-time, faraway friend, Sam Turner, had sent me an email. My eyes were glued to his message:

Dear Barbara,

With a new year starting soon, I was sitting here reminiscing about my "growing up" years and thought how blessed I was to grow up with your brothers and you. I remember that you, Phill, and Butch took me in when we moved into a nearby house. You helped me become a member of the neighborhood gang of other kids. I will never forget how your brothers found me an old broomstick, so I would have a horse to ride. We spent days herding cattle and chasing outlaws. What an imagination these two adventuresome guys awakened in me. Equally important, they protected me (and you!) from the neighborhood bullies and showed me how to stand up for myself. By example, they taught me how to share. Considered the rich kid in the neighborhood, I gained an understanding from your brothers

and you what real riches are. I will always be
grateful for those childhood years with you.

Your Friend,
Sam

With a hurting heart, I replied to Sam's email, telling him about Butch's death. Moments later, Sam called and began apologizing for sending his email, "What horrible timing for me to send you an email! I had no idea that Butch was sick, much less that he had died."

"Sam, your email is one of the most meaningful ones I will ever receive!" I exclaimed. "Few things surpass knowing that one's life brought happiness to someone else. Thank you very much for sending your email." After visiting briefly, we said our goodbyes. I have kept Sam's email and often re-read it, for it gives great comfort and peace, especially during the holidays.

Just as the wise men traveled from afar with gifts for the Christ child the first Christmas, my far-away friend wrote a divine message I desperately needed to hear on my younger brother's last Christmas. The wise men's timing was perfect, and so was Sam's!

Trading in Santa Claus

It is Christmas every time you let God love
others through you. It is Christmas every time
you smile at someone and offer your hand. It
is Christmas when you let God love you.

Mother Teresa

The Ladies' Annual Christmas Evening at my church is always a momentous occasion, so when I was asked to be the speaker, I readily accepted. The topic seemed simple enough: "When Did I Quit Believing in Santa Claus and Begin Understanding the Real Meaning of Christmas?" At times, I thought I had fully grasped the magnificence of Christmas only to have a new experience that influenced me to embrace the gifts of Christmas even more fully—and to "trade in" Santa Claus. Sharing a few of these pivotal experiences, I used these Christmas realities as my guideposts: *Love, Hope, Joy, Peace,* and *Faith.*

Love. As a youngster, I rather liked believing in Santa. I was not eager to give up the belief, or at least the pretense of believing, lest I miss out on the presents. My mother, grandmother, and grandfather did not simply talk about God or the religious aspects of Christmas. In contrast, they showed me what love was all about by their example as they served long hours seven days a week in my grandmother's café.

I have countless memories in that café, but one, in particular, stands out. My grandmother and I were returning to her café with kitchen supplies. Christmas shoppers loved the good food her café provided. The parking lot was full, and we had to park quite a distance from the café's back entrance. As we unloaded our supplies, we noticed a homeless man leaving an abandoned car, evidently his home for the night. He headed toward a garbage bin and began sifting through its contents and putting discarded food into his bag. My grandmother went directly to him and said, "Please come into my café. I want you to enjoy a hot meal."

As he reluctantly entered with her, she showed him to a table and asked the waitress to get him whatever he wanted to eat. A few "notable" businessmen known also for their church affiliations were seated nearby. One of the gentlemen jumped up and blurted out to my grandmother, "We are not eating here if you are going to feed the likes of him!"

My grandmother calmly responded, "He *is* going to eat here. I hope you and your friends will too." The self-appointed spokesperson stalked out along with a few stragglers from the group. Within a week, they all had returned, and so had the homeless man.

Love like that didn't come from Santa Claus. I knew that what I saw in the way my grandmother cared for people—not only at Christmas but throughout the year—was the real gift of Christmas.

> *Truly I tell you, whatever you did for one of the least of these brothers and sisters of mine, you did for me.*
> Matthew 25:40 (NIV)

Hope. California was my destination! The long drive from my home state of New Mexico to attend grad school was exhausting but made me even more eager to get started. I loved my classes because my classroom professors were excellent, and the subjects were intriguing.

Other aspects of my graduate studies and campus life, however, were a miserable contrast. The professor directing my program was an alcoholic, and she tended to be short-tempered and unpredictable. The hippie movement of the sixties and the Haight-Ashbury drug culture were very active. In addition, the Free Speech Movement of 1964 and 1965 was rampant on the Berkeley campus and obvious on the Stanford campus. Usually, I could avoid the disruptive crowds, but in December 1964, I was studying for final exams and trying to get through thousands of protesting students to go to the library. I heard snippets of Mario Savio's historic speech, but the unruly protestors were frightening to me. I prayed for God's help in coping with the professor and getting into the library safely that day.

As I rode the train back to New Mexico for Christmas break, my young mind tried to sort out what I had experienced and seen. I knew I wanted an approach to life that was better than most of what I had witnessed. That was a turning point; neither a superficial Santa nor drugs or otherworldly forces would satisfy my search. Only God could provide the source of that kind of *hope*—another gift of Christmas.

> *For I know the plans I have for you…*
> *to give you hope and a future.*
> Jeremiah 29:11 (NIV)

Joy. Working with women in Africa was part of my teaching and research appointment at the University of Nebraska. On one assignment in Nigeria, I worked with a professor who had received her PhD from the University of Nebraska. As my friend Dorcas and I visited the villages during the holidays, I saw the sheer joy in everything the women did as Christmas approached. These women lived in very spartan conditions and had very few material possessions. Their Christmas gift-giving was a drop in the bucket compared with the frenzy of gifts we, Americans, are accustomed to. They sang Christmas carols with genuine joy, they interacted with each other with joy, and they loved their children with overflowing joy.

Dorcas's two daughters had accompanied her to Nebraska and spent three years in their temporary home. Because I had become acquainted with the daughters while they were in Nebraska, I was happy to see them again in Nigeria. One evening I asked them if they missed living in the United States. I was expecting quite a different response from what I heard. The oldest daughter spoke first, "No, I don't miss the United States." The younger one shook her head in agreement and then added, "It's a nice place to visit…but I wouldn't want to live there." Dorcas and I later talked about their responses. "My daughters love the emphasis on relationships in our country, not possessions."

Working with these women and their daughters gave me even greater insight into another wonderful gift of Christmas: *joy.*

> *You have made known to me the paths of life;*
> *you will fill me with joy in your presence.*
> Acts 2:28 (NIV)

Peace. My mother remarried several years after my father was killed, and she had three daughters. The youngest, Janet, and her husband were killed by a drunk driver. At the driver's trial, the judge pronounced him guilty of two counts of negligent homicide and guilty as a habitual criminal. After the trial, my mother went to the mother of the man who had killed Janet and said to her, "I am so sorry." The mother said to my mother, "How can you ever forgive my son?" Without hesitation, my mother said, "I feel very sorry for your son and am going to pray for him." When I asked my mother how she could forgive someone who had killed her daughter, she answered, "I am heartbroken about losing Janet, but I am also heartbroken for that mother." Forgiving was the only way she could face the holiday season. It was the only path she could have to *peace*, another gift of Christmas.

Peace I leave with you; my peace I give you. I do not give to you as the world gives. Do not let your hearts be troubled.
John 14:27 (NIV)

Faith. By the end of the last semester in my doctoral program, the flu pandemic of 1968 had killed one million worldwide and about 100,000 in the United States. Because I was busy completing my dissertation, I had not paid much attention to the pandemic. That is, until I became ill with the flu. I was four to five months pregnant with our first baby, so I had a reason for concern. I had begun to feel better when Del became ill. After he went to bed to rest, I was struck by unbearable pain. The unrelenting pain intensified, so I woke Del. "We are going to the hospital!" he said.

As soon as we reached the hospital, I was wheeled to surgery and did not remember much until I woke up to the sounds of babies crying. I saw a mother walking, holding her newborn. I knew I'd lost my baby, so the sounds and sights were overwhelming. I asked a nurse who had come into my room, "Where is my husband?"

She answered, "The doctor sent him home; he is ill, and he doesn't need to be around new babies."

My heart wanted to scream out, "I do not need to be around new babies either!" I learned before leaving the hospital that a minimum number of staff members was working because of the Christmas holidays; this is why I was put on the wing with the newborns. I did not begrudge the other women and their new babies; however, I was devastated by the premature loss of mine.

Anywhere in the hospital would have been easier on the raw grief gnawing at my heart. Never had I felt so alone and heartsick. We had no family within hundreds of miles. Most of my friends had gone home for the Christmas break, and others did not know what had happened. I curled into a fetal position under the cold, sterile, white sheets and felt I could only dream of a miserable Christmas.

As I lay there waiting for sleep to come, my thoughts turned to the first Christmas. Nearly two thousand years ago, Mary was given a baby she had not planned on having. I had lost a baby I had not planned on losing. Her baby would give us Christmas and all its gifts: love, hope, joy, peace, and faith. What a Christmas! My heart was touched in a way that had never happened to me before. In that moment, as I was alone in that hospital room, the presence of God was never more real.

Every year since, the Christmas story reminds me of a God who gives more than I can fathom. While much of the world is enthralled with Santa Claus and his bag of toys, I am amazed by the thought that it is Christ who gives us all the gifts we need to cope with whatever comes our way. Certainly, the idea of Santa would brighten any child's face. But for me as an adult, I'll trade that any day for the gifts Christ gives. From that cold, lonely hospital room, I left without a baby in my arms, but I brought home a stronger belief in God that has neither faltered nor disappointed. It was in the midst of sickness, loss, and heartbreak that I was thrown into the arms of God. It was in the midst of the death of a dream that the Christmas gift of *faith* came alive, and from faith, God gradually embraced me even more fully with His other gifts—love, hope, joy, and peace.

Be still, and know that I am God.
Psalm 46:10 (NIV)

PART TWO

CELEBRATING THE GIFTS
OF HOPE AND PEACE

Delayed Delivery

Love leaves a memory
No one can steal
(from a headstone in Ireland)

Loaded down with luggage and doubt, Carol drove off in her car. The trip was inevitable. She was leaving a house that had been home for the last fifteen years. Her twenty-one-year marriage had ended abruptly in an unexpected, unwanted divorce. The thought of her two teenage children choosing to stay with their father and his new wife cut painfully through her already aching heart. They were, however, within one and three years of graduating high school with many friends they had known since kindergarten. They did not know anyone their ages in Virginia. Reluctantly, Carol agreed to their decision.

After a hot, exhausting two-day trip from Missouri to Virginia, Carol pulled into her sister's driveway. On the front lawn, three people were engaged in a friendly conversation: Carol's sister, one of her sister's neighbors, and a man Carol did not know. Because of the unseasonal heat, Carol asked if she could quickly take a few items into the house.

The neighbor introduced her congenial nephew. "Rick is more like a son," she said with obvious affection. The expression on her face turned sad as she added, "My only child was killed as a young adult in an auto crash." After a few seconds of silence, Rick said with a smile, "Let's get your other things unloaded."

Carol recalled what she had learned while her new acquaintance helped unload her car. Rick was an officer in the military and often stationed in faraway places but had come to see his elderly aunt as frequently as possible. He would be retiring within the year and promised his aunt he would return soon. The Good Samaritan had to leave early the morning after meeting Carol. "Too early for me to help you with your luggage when you move," he kidded.

After a few days, Carol moved into her new home and then totally immersed herself in her new position at the university she had graduated from and had grown to love even more as the years went by. She wanted to resume a normal life after struggling to recover from a failed marriage and an excruciating divorce.

About three months after Carol moved to Virginia, her assistant called to tell her a gentleman would like to see her for a few minutes. "His name is Rick," her assistant explained. Carol was just about to say, "I do not know anyone named Rick," when her heart fluttered. "Could it be *that* Rick?" she said to herself. Carol replied in the most professional voice she could manage, "Please show him the way to my office."

When Rick came into Carol's office, they both broke into heartfelt smiles. The spark between them continued to light up their conversation. Rick explained that he would be spending several days at a nearby aerospace operation.

Although Carol was loving every minute of talking with her unannounced visitor, she reminded herself that she was not looking for another relationship. Because the emotional wounds from her former husband's unfaithfulness had not healed, Carol was hesitant to expose her heart to possible hurt again. But as Rick rose from his chair and prepared to leave, Carol blurted out, "Our neighborhood association is having a potluck dinner tomorrow evening. Why don't you go with me to it?"

Rick quickly replied, "That sounds great. I would like to." He added, "What can I bring?"

Carol replied, "Just your appetite."

Laughing, he said, "No problem, I can bring lots of that."

The next evening "worked well," as Carol expressed it. After that, Carol and Rick's friendship flourished. "Rick's warm and caring companionship began weaving itself into the fabric of my life," she explained. Early in their dating, Carol read this definition somewhere: "True love is a friendship that caught fire."

"I realized this was happening with Rick and me. Getting married finally just seemed right." Carol took great joy in sharing how Rick told one of their friends, "I had a deep feeling that I had loved Carol all my life, long before we met. I had always dreamed of meeting and loving someone like her."

Rick and Carol's relationship was a solid friendship that fueled a warm atmosphere in their home life. Carol reminisced, "We loved each other dearly. Our life was rich and full. We had friends; Rick was quickly accepted by all my university colleagues and my family." Carol concluded, "Rick finally had the family—wife, kids, and grandkids—he had always longed for, and our love was mutual. We frequently said to each other, '*Love* and *more love*.'"

But the perfect course of their life together was about to change directions dramatically. Rick was diagnosed with cancer, followed by surgery. Having received a positive prognosis, "We were ecstatic," Carol said after the surgery. Rick remained cancer-free for more than a year. But then the terrifying symptoms and the exhausting tests and treatment resumed.

The next months were unpredictable and unsettling, physically and emotionally. Each reprieve would be followed by yet another frightening development. The ravages of cancer won, and the unthinkable happened—Rick died. Carol recalled, "Although I was exhausted, I was at peace. Together we fought the battle with all our love, strength, and prayers. All was not lost, for we had shared nine wonderful years together." She added, "I did not know of the battles of loneliness yet to be fought."

"That first Thanksgiving without Rick was unbearable," Carol recounted. With that prelude, she dreaded the Christmas holidays. Carol's heart only became heavier as the season inched toward Christmas Day. Her children and grandchildren had grown to love this tall, friendly Virginian and looked forward to special holiday visits with him. He had a way of lighting up any occasion. Her daughter, son-in-law, and grandchildren were driving from Missouri to Virginia for the holidays. They would stay at the home of Carol's sister because it was large enough to accommodate their growing family. For Carol to have to go to her sister's home without Rick to celebrate Christmas was going to add to her holiday agony.

A few days before Christmas, an old friend of Rick's called to ask Carol if she had just a few minutes to spare him. Carol quickly agreed and told him, "Come on over. I am in my 'crying clothes' and would love a visit from any of Rick's friends."

When Carol opened the front door, she and Rick's friend embraced. They began recollecting the good times they had enjoyed with their mutual friend. After nearly an hour of an engaging conversation, a comfortable quietness embraced them.

The silence was broken when the guest said, "Here." Handing Carol a small beautifully wrapped package, he continued, "Rick had this finished by June, but he wanted you to have a special Christmas gift from him." After a pause, he added, "So this gift is from Rick."

When Carol began opening it, she simply could not imagine what it could be. As she peeled the final layer of wrapping paper away and opened the box, her heart fluttered. In the box was a beautiful gold ring with nine sparkling diamonds mounted on it.

"Rick designed the ring himself," the friend explained. "The nine diamonds are for each of the nine years you and Rick had together." His kind voice continued, "The inscription is to remind you every day of the love you two shared." Carol read the words aloud: "*Love and More Love.*" A warm serenity filled Carol as she slipped the ring on her finger.

After the friend left, Carol sat down in Rick's chair, the chair where Rick should have been sitting. Her heart still ached as she curled up there, but not as terribly as it had since Rick's death. She held up her hand so she could look at her beautiful ring with its nine sparkling diamonds.

Leaving Missouri eleven years ago, Carol had wondered if she'd ever find happiness again. Her life with Rick vanquished that doubt. He had given her courage to face life's setbacks and go on searching for—and enjoying—the good things in life.

Still settled in Rick's chair, Carol took a long, deep breath and pressed the speed dial on her phone to call her sister. When her sister answered, Carol announced with a touch of cheer that had long been absent in her voice, "I am looking forward to Christmas with everyone at your house this year!"

Christmas would never be the same, but it could still be good. Rick's beautiful gift, with its delayed delivery, was the perfect gift at the perfect time.

Cinderella's Surprise

So do not fear, for I am with you; do not
be dismayed, for I am your God.
I will strengthen you and help you; I will uphold
you with my righteous right hand.

Isaiah 41:10 (NIV)

Cinderella was the part I wanted in the class play when I was in the fifth grade. Right before Christmas break, our teacher invited students to select the roles they wanted, and a class vote would determine who would play each part. We would have the holiday break to memorize our lines.

"The Cinderella-type" did not exactly describe me, for I was an all-out tomboy, with windblown hair and skinned knees from rough and tumble outdoor skirmishes with my brothers. But these were the very reasons I wanted to play Cinderella. I was ready to make a change. I was ready to be a princess! When the votes were counted, it was a wonderful surprise to learn I had more votes than anyone else to be Cinderella.

Jubilant, I could hardly wait to announce my new fame to my mother, grandmother, and grandfather. Busy as they were with their jobs, they shared my excitement and couldn't wait to watch the performance. Every neighbor I could find also congratulated me. "Being Cinderella will be the best Christmas gift ever," I told myself.

My joy was short-lived. When the class began the next day, the teacher asked me to come to her desk. She minced no words. "After thinking about it—" she began. As she turned her eyes away from me, she made a shattering pronouncement, "I believe you are better suited for another role." This was not such a wonderful surprise.

The clock struck midnight in my heart. I felt like I had been banished to sweeping ash and soot for the rest of my life.

Dejected, I trudged home for Christmas break. My family, friends, and neighbors offered encouragement. One said, "Life is not always fair. Find a way to overcome." A caring neighbor offered, "Show the teacher—and prove to yourself—that you can rise above the unfair way she handled the situation." Another provided this brief but constructive advice: "Make the best of it." One of my friends and competitive classmates challenged me to be a great wicked stepmother, the role the teacher had chosen for me.

Of all the advice given to me, perhaps the best was from an older lady who lived down the street. She wrote something on a card, handed it to me, and said, "Read this." I read her paraphrase of Isaiah 41:10: "Do not be afraid. I am your God, and I will help you." She looked me straight in the eye and said with heartfelt emotion: "Read this over and over again to remind yourself that God is with you and will help you do your very best."

All the well-meaning advice was taken to heart. Before long, I was enjoying learning and practicing my lines. This came as a surprise to my family and my friends, and to me! Never had I felt such a sense of purpose or joy doing homework during the Christmas holidays. By the time school resumed, I had not only memorized my lines, but I had also practiced them with emotion-packed drama.

As the time for the performance grew nearer, I felt the anticipation of a princess going to a fairy tale ball. The curtain rose, and we gave the performance of our fifth-grade lives. After the show, my heart swelled as the audience stood to their feet with applause. Classmates, teachers, parents, grandparents, and others raved about how well the cast performed.

Through that childhood experience, the seeds were sown for an unwavering faith that God would help me in all kinds of trouble and make the best of bad situations. Looking back, I wonder if the gift of *not* playing Cinderella might have been one of the best surprises ever.

Remembering Julie

It matters not how long we live, but how we live.

Francis Bailey

Julie was one of my all-time favorite students at any of the universities where I taught. Warm, friendly, attractive, energetic, gifted. That described Julie. She was a delightful person and an ideal student.

I remember our last conversation. When it was time for the class to be over, most of the students left to grab lunch at the student union. But Julie remained. She visited with several students until I finished talking to another student. When it was her turn to talk to me, she asked questions about the upcoming exam. She had obviously already done some serious studying. Several other students overheard her questions and joined our conversation. Julie's winsome personality drew people to her.

Julie never made it to the exam. Later that day, she was riding her bike when she was tragically struck by a truck at a busy intersection near campus. I was stunned when one of Julie's friends came by my office and told me the devastating news. I could not believe what I had heard! Only hours before, twenty-year-old Julie was talking with friends, laughing, making plans for the future, and studying for the exam in my human development class. But now, Julie lay unconscious and motionless in a hospital across town from the campus. My heart cried out to her. *You cannot die, Julie! You're every professor's dream—and every parent's. You have so much to offer, so much to live for.*

Throughout the afternoon, nurses silently came and went from Julie's hospital room. Her parents stood nearby in quiet desperation. The attending physician entered the room, cleared his throat, and said to Julie's parents and her two brothers, "Your Julie has only a few hours to live." Because he knew the parents, he felt the freedom to ask, "Would you consider donating some of Julie's organs?" Silence filled the room.

At that same moment in a neighboring state, Mary, a young mother, squinted her eyes and leaned forward, struggling to see her lively two-year-old. Mary was going blind and was storing up memories to savor when she could no longer see her young child.

Several states away, Jon had almost finished six hours on the dialysis machine. This young father was reading to his two sons while his immobilized body was connected to a life-giving "artificial kidney." Doctors had given him the grim prognosis of only weeks to live. His only hope was a kidney transplant.

Meanwhile, in the Lincoln, Nebraska hospital, Julie's grief-stricken parents pondered the finality of the physician's question. Their pretty brunette, brown-eyed daughter had once said she wanted to be an organ donor in the event of her death. The two parents looked at each other briefly, the anguish in the hearts reflected in their eyes. Then they turned to the physician as Julie's father responded, "Yes. Julie always gave to others while she was alive." Julie's mother added, "She would want to give in death."

Within twenty-four hours, Mary was notified that she would receive one of Julie's eyes, and John was told to start preparing for a kidney transplant. Julie's other eye and organs would give life and sight to additional waiting recipients.

"Julie died right after her twentieth birthday," her mother told me some years later. She continued, "Her life was a gift to us. Knowing that in her death, she gave the gift of life and sight to others is comforting to us. Carrying out her wishes has helped us cope with her death more than anything else."

I remember finishing the semester that Julie was in my human development and behavior class. I was reviewing my gradebook to calculate final grades before the Christmas holidays. The place for a final grade was blank after Julie's name. No grade, of course, would need to be written there. I stared at Julie's name as I thought how she would have loved celebrating the Christmas season with her family and friends, how she had lived her life so fully, how she was a friend to all. How she did her best in everything she attempted in life. How being an organ donor gave new life to others. Julie knew how to live, and she knew how to die. *That's what "human development and behavior" is all about,* I thought to myself. With no hesitation, I put by Julie's name:

Final Grade: A+

A Message from Emily

And now these three remain: faith, hope and
love. But the greatest of these is love.
1 Corinthians 13:13 (NIV)

Emily scrunched up her face as she carefully printed three
words on a small piece of wrinkled paper:

Next, she drew a heart around her words. Satisfied with what she saw, the young girl carefully folded the paper and skipped into the kitchen where her mother was preparing dinner. Without a word, Emily handed the note to her mother. Nancy read the note, smiled, and gave her young daughter a hug and kiss and an enthusiastic, "Thank you!"

Grateful for the note, Nancy tucked it into one of the pockets of her cable knit sweater and resumed stirring her steaming pot of homemade soup. Having moved from the warmer climate of Texas, her family was trying to adjust to the cooler weather in Northern California. Hot soup and warm sweaters helped.

Years later, Nancy and her family moved back to Texas. Nancy and I were in the same Bible class when I announced, "The residents of the nursing home where I volunteer need gently-worn clothing. We'll give them as gifts at their Christmas party." These residents have, as one person put it, "lasted longer than their money." These residents would be blessed by gifts at Christmas.

From a box of clothing she had worn in the cooler California climate, Nancy selected several items to donate, including the pretty cable knit sweater with two pockets. The sweater was a perfect gift for Miss Abby, a frail ninety-two-year-old who always complained of being cold. Knowing she would not be getting gifts from family members, I immediately tagged the sweater for Miss Abby, as her only daughter had died decades ago. Her two grandchildren grew up in a faraway state and had not contacted her in years. She had outlived all her other relatives.

At the Christmas party a week after Thanksgiving, Miss Abby took one look at the sweater. It was love at first sight, and it was a perfect fit! After the Christmas party, Miss Abby was still proudly wearing her sweater as a nurse's aide wheeled her back to her room.

Miss Abby was adamant about wearing her sweater, even at bedtime. Her aide kindly encouraged her to lay it on top of her covers, close to her face. This pacified Miss Abby at night, and during the day, she insisted on wearing the sweater.

Several days later, the aide told Miss Abby that her sweater must be cleaned. She searched the pockets before laundering the sweater. In one pocket, she found a small piece of pink paper. "What have we here?" the aide asked as she unfolded the paper.

Looking fearful, Miss Abby replied, "I don't know."

"Seems to be a note to you," the aide commented, and then read the note to Miss Abby:

I LOVE YOU

"Look," she said as she turned the note for Miss Abby to see, "a heart is drawn around the message to you." Miss Abby's face softened. Her eyes opened in surprise, and her mouth turned into a heartfelt smile. "Someone loves me?" she asked the nurse's aide.

Standing nearby, the quick-thinking aide answered, "Yes. The message must be to you. Someone does love you." Miss Abby reached out to the aide with an open hand. The aide put the note in her hand. Ever so gently, Miss Abby closed her hand and leaned back on her pillow. She looked happier than the aide could ever remember.

Emily was grown and had children of her own by now, but her thoughtful and spontaneous words as a youngster were divinely protected and delivered for Miss Abby's last Christmas. Gently cradling the cherished message in her hand and wearing her soft, warm sweater, Miss Abby died peacefully the day after Christmas, knowing that someone loved her.

The Best Christmas Eve Gift Ever

A brother is born to help in time of need.

Proverbs 17:17 (NLT)

When Phill was born on Christmas Eve, our parents knew he was a special Christmas gift. He was their firstborn, my brother, Butch, was born next, and I came along soon after Phill turned three. I couldn't have known then what a special life-long gift Phill would be to me.

I loved Phill because he was a lot of fun, smart, and kind to our brother Butch and me. My childhood was full of wonderful memories of Phill. My older brother taught his younger siblings how to catch frogs and snakes…and let them go back where they belonged. He helped us make forts from the blankets and sheets from our beds and get them back in place before our mother or grandmother came home from work. He taught us both how to read all the words in comic books before we could read anything else. Phill made sure we knew how to stay calm in a crisis, like when Butch and I caught the grass in our front lawn on fire with broom straws we had put in the open gas heater and taken outside to use like sparklers. Phill "kept his cool" as he grabbed the water hose and put out the fire before we burned the house down. Phill taught me so much. What a gift!

Phill enjoyed his early years filled with typical boyhood experiences: playing in the yard, riding bikes, spending hours in the city park's swimming pool, and going to the Saturday movie. The best part of his many activities was that I got to go along with him. One "activity" I thought was especially exciting was running across the corner of the pasture where the neighbors' cattle grazed. Mother repeatedly and emphatically warned us, "Stay out of the pasture where those bulls are."

As soon as our mother drove away from the house on her way to work, we headed for that pasture, as did other kids in the neighborhood. The bulls probably would not have been a threat to us, but some of the older boys would yell at the top of their lungs and run at them, getting as close as they dared. After so much commotion, at least one of the bulls would paw the earth and begin running toward us. My big brother Phill would always make sure he had a firm grip on my hand as we ran away from the agitated bulls back to the safety of the fence. Phill always protected me from danger. What a gift!

Some of my first lessons in considering others were taught to me by Phill. He said that I made his job of "watching out for me" almost impossible. He elaborated, "You wanted to be your own boss, but at times you just couldn't cut the mustard." Phill, for example, was supposed to make sure I ate breakfast and got dressed in time to arrive at school on time. Everything worked well until getting my shoes tied. I could not tie them, and I would not let Phill do it. Several times I arrived at school with shoes untied and shoelaces dragging in the dirt. Phill put his hands on my shoulders and looked me straight in the eye, "You are making me appear irresponsible. You are going to let me teach you how to tie your shoes, like it or not." I did not like it, but he did teach me to tie my shoes, and he did open my eyes to considering his feelings on the matter. What a gift!

My big brother Phill loved to learn, and he had a wide variety of interests, which he often shared with me. Photography was one of his special interests. As a youngster, he was the first one in the neighborhood to have his own camera; he had saved his meager allowance to buy a small Brownie camera.

He quickly mastered it and advanced to more sophisticated equipment. He said to me, "I would teach you how to use my Brownie camera and let you borrow it, but I don't think you'd take very good care of it." Another reason I loved my big brother: he was honest with me when he needed to be. Though I didn't always like that sort of honesty, I realize now what a gift it was!

Phill gave me many reasons to be proud of him. When in high school, he was a popular class member. His classmates voted him Freshman Favorite, Carnival King, and "Most Handsome." (These were all well-deserved honors, for he was very likable and good-looking!) Being modest about these honors was his characteristic reaction to his many strengths, abilities, and accomplishments. Phill's modesty set a good example for me and was yet another reason for my considering him a gift to me.

Phill was also a gift to our country, for he was a patriot in the truest sense of the word. He loved this country and committed to serving it by joining the U.S. Navy. He often quoted John F. Kennedy: "Any man who is asked what he did to make his life worthwhile, I think can respond with a good deal of pride and satisfaction if he can say: 'I served in the United States Navy.'"

While in the Navy, Phill served around the world, including Turkey, Germany, Washington, D.C., Hawaii, Guam, Formosa (Taiwan), California, Washington State, and the Philippines. Phill's professionalism and extraordinary competence were recognized by his "fast track" promotions and the men who served with him. For example, a shipmate said in an email: "Phill was a great man. It was a deep and genuine pleasure knowing a man I thought of as a mentor. His wit and wisdom were always greatly appreciated. I was blessed to have had the pleasure of knowing Phill as a shipmate and a friend."

Comments like this only added to my feeling that Phill, my big brother, was a true gift.

While in graduate school in California, I received a letter from Phill telling me that he and his wife and toddler Phillip Alan would be flying from the Philippines to an Air Force base near the university I was attending. He asked if I would like to ride to New Mexico with them. Their trip coincided perfectly with my week of spring break. The plan worked well until about 4:00 a.m. while I was taking my turn driving on a long stretch of highway in New Mexico. Suddenly the sound of slinging gravel, the uneven bumps off the edge of the road toward a steep ravine, and Phill's strong hands grabbing the steering wheel startled me. I had gone to sleep at the wheel! Had Phill not awakened immediately and taken control of our car, certain death or serious injuries would have been the fate of us all. While I felt terrible about the ordeal, Phill was kind and reassuring to me. Once again, Phill put into action the scripture, "A brother is born to help in time of need" (Proverbs 17:17, NLT).

Phill's sense of humor was often subtle and expressed in unexpected ways. He knew by memory many quotes of famous people and repeated them at just the right times in conversations. Phill's favorites tell a lot about him:

> "Better to remain silent and be thought a fool than to speak out and remove all doubt." (Abraham Lincoln)

> "Success is not final; failure is not fatal. It is the courage to continue that counts." (Winston S. Churchill)

> "There are those who imagine that the unlucky accidents of life—life's 'experi-

ences'—are in some way useful to us. I wish I could find out how. I never know one of them to happen twice. They always change off and swap around and catch you on your inexperienced side." (Mark Twain)

"I find the harder I work, the more luck I have." (Thomas Jefferson)

"Always do right. This will gratify some people and astonish the rest." (Mark Twain)

God gave His Son on the very first Christmas, and He was the perfect gift for us all. And God gave me the gift of my big brother Phill, and it couldn't be more perfect than to celebrate his birthday on Christmas Eve.

A Season for Sharing

There is a time for everything... A time
to weep, and a time to laugh.

Ecclesiastes 3:1, 4 (NIV)

Gladys was one of the most colorful residents of a local retirement center. One evening when she was sitting in the lobby enjoying looking at the Christmas tree, a young man came in the front door and sat down beside her.

Not saying anything, the young man began nibbling on the peanuts in a bowl on the table between Gladys and him. It was the holidays, and bowls of candy and other treats decorated the tables. Soon he began eating the peanuts by the handful. When he reached the bottom of the bowl and realized what he had done, he looked at Gladys remorsefully and said, "I apologize for eating all the peanuts, but they were so good."

"No apology needed, honey," Gladys quickly replied. Without taking her eyes off the Christmas tree, she continued, "That's okay. I don't like peanuts, just chocolate, and I had already sucked the chocolate off them. After all, Christmas is a season for sharing."[5]

Ice Angel

But when we cried out to the Lord, he
heard our cry and sent an angel.

Numbers 20:16 (NIV)

"You believe in angels, I am sure," a friend softly commented.
Raising her voice, she then asked, "But have you ever *seen* an
angel?"

It's funny how a simple question can snowball into an
avalanche of memories. One wintry incident rolled ahead of
the others. My friend listened eagerly as I relayed the story.

Exams for the fall semester had just ended. Our daughter,
Christi, was ten years old and was as happy as Del and I were
to be out of classes so we could begin celebrating the holidays.
Early one afternoon Christi and I decided the two of us would
drive into town and do our last-minute Christmas shopping.
At the time, we lived on an acreage six miles from the edge of
Lincoln, Nebraska. Winters could be treacherous in that part
of the world. One of my greatest fears was having a wreck on
the icy roads like one of my teaching colleagues: she was seriously injured and would be confined to a wheelchair for the
rest of her life. I checked the forecast. The temperature was
bitter cold, but no snow or ice was predicted.

Strolling leisurely through the mall and being part of the
congenial hustle and bustle of the other Christmas shoppers
was a sheer delight to Christi and me. Del was working all day
to finish his semester's grade reports. After making our pur-

chases and enjoying some hot chocolate, Christi and I headed for the exit onto the parking area into the sub-zero temperature. What a surprise—large, icy snowflakes were falling!

Just as I feared, the new-fallen snow made every surface it touched dangerously icy and slick. The streets were filled with cars slipping and sliding as they eased their way home. The highway home was even more perilous. Fear gripped me, and my hands gripped the steering wheel as I guided the car along the challenging six-mile stretch as carefully as I knew how. I would need to build up some speed to get over the first (and steepest) hill before turning off the highway onto the country road to our house. I accelerated as I approached the dreaded incline, but just before we reached the top, the tires lost all traction.

No other cars were behind us, so I let our car slide slowly backward until it stopped. After putting the car in park, I got out and placed large strips of carpet under my tires. (Many people carried strips of carpet in their cars for this very purpose.) This tactic got our car a little closer to the top of the hill, but again the car lost traction before reaching the top. I tried the carpet again, with no success.

Soon other cars were skidding and sliding on the icy highway approaching the top of the hill. Some people were helping push cars up the incline and over the hill; others roared on past those of us stalled, with great risk of colliding with someone coming over the hill from the other direction.

Del would become worried about us if he arrived at home and found us not there. It was before the arrival of cell phones, so I asked Christi to go to the nearby farmhouse and call Del at his office. First, we held hands and prayed for our safety and the safety of the many other stranded drivers. I continued to pray as I watched Christi trudge bravely through the snow.

As Christi returned and climbed back into the car, a pickup came over the hill from the opposite direction. In spite of many other cars spinning helter-skelter, the driver of the pickup pulled up alongside our car and shouted, "You ladies need some help?" Without hesitation, I replied, "We sure do." The stranger turned his pickup around and hooked a heavy chain from his truck to our car, and eased us over the hill.

As the mystery driver was disconnecting the chain, Del drove up alongside him. Seeing what had happened, Del called out to the man, "What do I owe you?" As the man turned his pickup around to drive back the same direction he had come, he called out, "Not a thing. Just have a Merry Christmas!" As my husband and the man exchanged these brief words, I carefully jotted down the Good Samaritan's license plate number in the hopes of thanking him later.

The day after Christmas, I called the Division of Motor Vehicles. When I explained that I wanted to thank the man for his kindness, the person answering the phone said she would ask her supervisor. This person came to the phone and told me he would have to contact the driver to ask if he could give me his name and phone number. I waited while he did some checking.

The supervisor came back to the phone and asked if I was sure of the license plate information I had given him. I emphasized how I had carefully written it and then double-checked it. I was certain I had copied it correctly! He then said to me, "There is no license plate with that number."

I was too stunned to say anything; the scene on top of that cold, icy hill flashed through my mind: how Christi and I prayed so hard and sincerely, how the man in that truck drove straight to our car as though he knew exactly where he was going, how he refused payment, how he waved good-bye and wished us a Merry Christmas, how he turned around and drove back the same way he had come—and how *I carefully wrote down his license plate number.* Breaking the silence, the supervisor said, "I am sorry I cannot help you."

At that point, my friend interrupted me, "Don't you wish he could've helped you?"

"He did help me!" I exclaimed. "Until that stranger appeared out of nowhere to rescue Christi and me, I had never seen an angel. But when that supervisor could find no record of his license plate, I knew I had seen an angel!"

Celebrating Wade

Weeping may last through the night, but
joy comes with the morning.

Psalm 30:5 (NLT)

"Bye, Mom!" Wade shouted as he straightened his baseball cap
and jumped into the car with his dad. "Wade was happy," my
friend, Nelda, said. Then she continued, "He was going with
his dad to Oshkosh, Wisconsin, for the national fly-in. My son
loved interacting with his dad and other airplane enthusiasts.
Wade was a great kid. But he was all boy, and he loved to wear
his baseball cap."

Nelda continued, "My life could not have been better."
She explained, "Larry and I had the perfect family, a boy and
a girl." My friend sighed, "I will never forget how my twelve-
year-old Wade looked in his baseball cap on July 25, 1991,
when he and his dad left for Wisconsin. They flew into unexpected bad weather. Neither of them survived the fiery crash."
Nelda added, "I lost two of the three people I loved most. My
life would never be the same."

A few weeks after the crash, a representative from the
Federal Aviation Administration came to Nelda's house and
told her the debris of the tragic accident had been taken to
Air Salvage in Lancaster, Texas. The only air salvage place for
private planes in the United States was just a few miles from
Nelda's house. Arrangements were made for her to go there to
try to find some of Larry's and Wade's personal items. A kind

and soft-spoken man greeted her and accompanied her to the large bins that held the remaining debris from the crash site. As Nelda stared at the bins, she voiced a prayer; more than anything, she wanted to find Wade's cap. Within a few minutes, the man asked, "Is this what you're looking for?" He was holding Wade's cap!

"At times, I felt so alone. Gripping Wade's cap, I whispered a prayer for God to help me," Nelda told me. She went on to explain how she found herself holding Holly close to her in the days and weeks to follow. She did not want to lose her daughter as she had lost her son and husband.

Nelda shared how God answered other prayers as she struggled with debilitating grief. She continued, "As the first Christmas after their deaths approached, powerful waves of grief drowned me. I dreaded the Christmas holidays. Thinking about the celebration, joy, and family togetherness I'd be missing that Christmas plunged me back into the anguish I'd felt immediately after the crash."

"One evening when I was praying—and holding Wade's cap, my prayer to be able to get through the first Christmas was beginning to be answered," Nelda told me. She explained that in March prior to Larry and Wade's death, they had spent time at a lodge in the Texas hill country. It was a place filled with wonderful memories. It was the last time they were all together on a vacation. Nelda desperately wanted—needed— an extended family that year. Nelda felt that loving family members surrounding and embracing them was the only way she and Holly could get through the Christmas holidays.

"Before I lost my courage," Nelda said, "I called the lodge." Gripping the phone, the young mother's knuckles turned white as she waited for someone to answer her call. Finally, the owner of the lodge answered the phone. "Please," Nelda pleaded, "could you find some way to make your lodge available this Christmas?" Through her tears, Nelda explained the circumstances the best she could. The silence on the other end of the phone seemed to last forever. The woman replied hesitantly that she had already promised the employees that she was closing the lodge so they could spend the holidays with their families. "But," she said, "give me a little while to do some checking. I will call you back." Nelda heaved a hopeful sigh and began praying for a miracle.

Less than thirty minutes later, the phone rang. Hands shaking, Nelda picked up the phone, "Hello." The owner of the lodge exclaimed, "My employees want to cook Christmas dinner for you and your family—and meals the days before and after Christmas Day."

Nelda explained, "They were willing for us to stay at the lodge, as long as we didn't mind serving ourselves while we were there. Of course, we didn't mind!" The staff prepared meals in advance and made the lodge a wonderful, warm place for the family to spend that first Christmas. "The love the staff of that lodge showed us was like a miracle." She elaborated, "That first Christmas was still hard, but they all helped us get through it. Just like we came to stay at the lodge that year, hope came to stay in our hearts."

After a few years, Nelda remarried, and they moved to another town when Holly was in the sixth grade. Nelda commented, "I saw God's hand in so many areas of our lives." She explained that on the first day of her new school, Holly met her best "forever friend," who, a number of years later, would introduce Holly to her future husband. They married and started a family of their own.

I bumped into Nelda one day at the airport in the town where we both then lived. Nelda was running toward me with a Texas-sized smile on her face. "I have just returned from helping Holly with her new baby," Nelda said. Catching her breath and smiling, she happily announced, "His name is Wade!"

As Nelda glowed about her new grandson, I thought about the long hours she spent holding Wade's baseball cap and praying and asking God to help them survive their loss. Her prayer was still being answered all these years later. Interrupting my thoughts, Nelda said, "Holly told me when little Wade is old enough, she is going to get him a baseball cap just like her brother wore."

Still smiling, Nelda said, "God is good."

Seeing Christmas

Worse than not having sight is having no vision.

Helen Keller

My day started out rotten. I overslept and was late for the graduate class I was teaching at Mills College in Oakland, California.
Things were going downhill. After teaching my class, I needed
to leave immediately to attend the graduate course I was taking. The students were obviously disgruntled, and so was I.

Everything that happened at school that day only aggra-
vated my nervous frenzy. It was cold and cloudy, and by
the time I reached the bus stop for my homeward trip, my
head pounded, and my stomach was in knots. Despite hearing Christmas music and seeing decorations everywhere, no
Christmas spirit stirred in me at all.

As usual, the bus was late and jam-packed. I had to stand
in the aisle and hang on for dear life, which is not easy for a 5'1"
person like I am. As the over-crowded, lurching bus hurled me
in all directions, my gloom deepened.

Then I heard a voice coming from the front of the bus,
"Beautiful day, isn't it?" Because of the crowd, I could not see
the man. But I heard him as he continued to comment on the
wintry scenery, calling attention to the colorful Christmas decorations of each approaching landmark: this bridge, that park,
this firehouse, that church. Soon all the passengers were gazing
happily out the windows. The man's unbridled enthusiasm was
so genuine that I found myself smiling.

The bus finally reached my stop. As I squeezed my way to the front of the bus, I got a look at our "guide" seated there, an older gentleman with a beard, wearing dark glasses and carrying a thin, wooden cane.

As it turns out, this blind man was seeing Christmas more richly and beautifully than I was that day. I'm so thankful he helped open my eyes to the joyous sights and beauty of Christmas. Sometimes the blind really do lead the blind.[6]

Needed: a Dozen Miracles

More things are wrought by prayer than this world dreams of.
Alfred Lord Tennyson

The stress and demands on police officers and the increasing number of officers killed in the line of duty keep even the most committed, courageous of them from completing thirty-five years of service—but not Frank Gentsch. When reaching that momentous year serving on the Waco, Texas, police force, Frank commented, "Reaching this milestone was not easy." He told the story of being shot and nearly killed as a young officer. "Living to see another Christmas," Frank said, "didn't look promising."

With tubes jutting out of his unresponsive body and countless needles jabbing him, Frank recalls thinking, *Is this what dying is like?* Bright lights reflected the seriousness of the situation. A steady stream of unfamiliar sounds in the ICU room added to the grave atmosphere. As doctors and nurses hovered over him, Frank slipped in and out of consciousness.

Anxious police officers crowded together in a nearby room. Towering above them, Chief of Police Larry Scott leaned his 6'6" frame toward them and looked straight into their distraught faces. Choking with emotion, Chief Scott whispered hoarsely, "It's going to take *a dozen miracles* to pull Frank through."

Ever since he was a young boy, Frank had dreamed of being a policeman. He looked forward to the day when he would be called "Officer Gentsch." Graduation from the Waco, Texas, Police Academy on October 1, 1981, fulfilled Frank's dream. On June 7, 1982, he celebrated his twentieth birthday. "On top of the world" is how Frank later described his feelings on June 19, 1982, as he made his rounds in a bad area of town.

The day was blistering hot. When Frank saw a fellow shuffling along in a heavy raincoat on a hot, sunny day, Frank knew he needed to check out such suspicious behavior.

Stepping out of his patrol car, Frank told the man, "Hey, I need to talk to you." Ignoring Frank, the man walked faster. More emphatically, Frank commanded, "Stop right now. I need to talk to you!" When Frank saw him put his hand inside his coat, he asked, "What do you have there?"

"A gun," the man growled as he swirled and pointed a large, shiny revolver straight at Frank and opened fire. The first bullet hit Frank's right arm. Frank knew this, not because of any pain, but because he could see the big hole the bullet had ripped in his arm. The next bullet drove into Frank's chest, right below his shirt pocket. Again, the young police officer must have been in shock because he felt no distress or discomfort.

"Getting shot isn't so bad," Frank thought, but then he saw the red blood oozing out of his chest onto his blue shirt. As blood saturated his shirt, memories flashed through his mind of officers wounded or killed during his time on the force. The question raced through Frank's mind, *Am I going to be next?*

The gunman darted into a deserted building. Other police officers responded quickly to Frank's call for help, several arriving on the scene almost immediately. After several horror-filled minutes, the ordeal was over.

Chief Scott pointed out later, "The police searched the assailant and found that he had seventy-six live rounds of .22-caliber ammunition in his possession, enough to kill all the officers who came to Frank's aid and every spectator the shootout attracted."

Amazingly, the gunman hit only two people, Frank, and another officer, who was shot in the leg. The other officer healed quickly and was soon back on the job, but Frank remained in the hospital for seventy days, playing a precarious game of tag with life and death.

"I learned a lot about life from my brush with death. I had lots of time to think," Frank commented later. With a smile on his face and resolve in his voice, he added, "Ironically, my being shot made me even more certain than ever that I wanted to be a policeman. I could hardly wait to get back on the job."

Frank returned to limited duty on September 10, 1982. A month later, he was supervising the new cadets. "When December rolled around, I began looking forward to Christmas," Frank said, "One reason was that I knew I would return to full duty in the Patrol Division just after the New Year. Mainly, though, I rejoiced at being alive to celebrate another Christmas." The doctors marveled at Frank's miraculous survival and concluded that his determination helped him survive multiple major surgeries and several close encounters with death.

Decades later, and currently, the Assistant Chief of Police, Frank commented, "We share gifts at Christmas to celebrate the miracle birth. Gifts I received that year strengthened my determination to live to celebrate another Christmas: prayers of family and friends, the expertise of the doctors, and countless acts of kindness."

Or, in the words of Chief Scott, those gifts were the *dozen miracles* that pulled Frank through. "I understand this better each year," Frank commented, "especially at Christmastime."

I Will Save a Place for You

Friends come and friends go, but a true
friend sticks by you like family.

Proverbs 18:24 (MSG)

"I will save a place for you." First spoken to me more than forty years ago, these words remind me of heartwarming experiences with Terry Scott. She and I had just met. Her husband, Dean of the School of Business at Baylor University, had offered my husband a position in the Accounting Department. While discussing our move to Waco, I lamented to Terry, "I left good friends and don't know anyone in Waco." After inviting me to a Baylor function, Terry added those reassuring words that launched a longstanding friendship.

Terry saved a place at the Baylor function not only for me but also for my husband and hers. At the end of the evening, Terry announced, "The next rendezvous is for ladies only." I asked Terry who would be there, and she quickly answered, "An assortment of easy-to-like ladies!"

Indeed they were! "Thank you," I said to my newfound friend, "for gathering this group for lunch."

With a fun-loving twinkle in her eye, Terry replied, "My husband told me that for the past twenty-five or so years, you attended school or taught school in various states and several foreign countries. So, I knew it would take some extra special women to convert you to 'a Texas lady.'"

Dreadful news came soon after that luncheon. My twenty-year-old sister and her husband were looking forward to eating out with friends. As they drove along the highway and approached their destination, a drunk driver ran a stop sign. The horrific collision killed my sister instantly. Her husband lived a few hours. Before the nine-hour trip to join my grief-stricken mother and other family members, I notified the choir director of our church that our daughter would not be participating in the youth choir musical. Word spread quickly about our tragedy. Terry Scott's call was the first: "What can we do to help?" Next, she called others, some I knew from the luncheon and a few I had not even met. Their assistance was invaluable before our sad trip and after our return. Terry and these other ladies made me want to be a "Texas lady!"

Terry's behind-the-scenes help was first apparent in the "Texas lady" situation, and that attitude was reflected throughout our friendship. Because my home state was New Mexico, I was asked to review the book *Death Comes for the Archbishop*. When I mentioned my "assignment" to Terry, she exclaimed, "I love that book!" Because the Scotts frequently traveled in New Mexico, I suspected that she was familiar with the "lay of the land" where this story took place. I asked her to help me. As usual, not wanting to be center stage, she emphasized, "As long as I do not have to say anything." The results? Several poster boards beautifully illustrating important points of the book. But the best one was a well-illustrated map displaying the travels and ministry of this priest from France who became the first Catholic bishop in the American territory of New Mexico.

On the day of the book review, I got stuck in traffic. I sent Terry a text. She replied, "I am here. I will save a place for you." When I arrived, Terry had everything set up. Of course, she did! The presentation was received with eager applause.

Rather than Christmas cards, Terry sent an annual Thanksgiving message of gratitude. If I could send a message to Terry, this is what I would say: "Terry, I am thankful for your genuineness and sincere friendship across decades, your eagerness to help in any situation, for your faith-filled life. This year I will miss your Thanksgiving message and our Christmas time together, but I am grateful for God's promise of heaven to those who believe. I can hear you whispering to me: 'I will save a place for you.'"

A Light in the Window

Heaven's light forever shines.

Percy Blythe Shelley

I love Christmas traditions! One of my favorites is the placing of lights in windows, for it reminds me of a story that has become even more meaningful as death increasingly claims my friends and relatives, and my "advancing" age forces me to face my own mortality.

Born in England in 1763, John Todd was only six years old when his father and mother died. Soon after he was orphaned and left all alone, he received a letter from his aunt living a long distance away. Although she had never met him, she wrote, "John, come live with me. I'm your aunt. I love you. I'll be your mother and father."

Instead of going to an orphanage, John went to live with his aunt. Because she was wealthy, she gave him advantages he would never have had. After attending the university, John moved away to attain a theological education. He worked hard and distinguished himself as a clergyman, librarian, and scholar. One day when he was forty-one years old, he received a letter from his aunt that said, "John, you know I don't write a letter unless it's important...so you know this is important." She continued, "The doctor tells me I have a terminal illness and shall soon die. I'm no scholar like you, John. What do you think I can expect?"

John wrote back to his aunt, and his letter has become a classic piece of literature. The letter is entitled:

"The Letter of a Little Boy of Six,
Written 35 Years Later"

Dear Auntie,

It is now thirty-five years since I, a little boy of six, was left alone in the world. You sent me word that you would give me a home and be a kind mother to me. I've never forgotten the day when I made that long journey to your house. I can still recall my disappointment when I learned that instead of coming for me yourself, you sent your hired man to fetch me. I can still remember my tears as, perched on a horse, I clung tightly to the back of your hired man, and we started trotting off to my new home.

Night fell before we finished the journey. As the darkness deepened, I began to be afraid. I said to the man in front of me, "Do you think she'll go to bed before I get there?" And he said, throwing his head back to me as the horse trotted on, "Oh no. She'll surely stay up for you, Johnny. When we get out of these woods, you'll see her candle lighted up presently."

As we rode into a clearing, there, sure enough, I did see a friendly candle in the window. I remember that you were waiting in the doorway. You put your arms around me, a tired, frightened little lad, and lifted me down from the horse.

I remember there was a bright fire with a hearth and a warm supper on the stove. After supper, you took me up to my room and heard me say my prayers. Then you sat beside me until I fell asleep. You're probably wondering why I'm recalling all of this now, Auntie. Well, your letter reminded me of it. For one day soon, God will send for you to take you to your new home. Don't fear the summons, or the strange journey, or the messenger. At the end of the road, you'll see a light in the window, and standing in the doorway, smiling to welcome you, will be Jesus. You will be safe forevermore. Auntie, God can be trusted to be as kind to you as you were to me thirty-five years ago.

Love,
John

When I read John Todd's words, I imagine his aunt reading those same words and breathing a deep sigh of comfort, becoming wrapped in divine peace, as if in a warm, soft blanket.

For decades I have written about the death and grief of others, but now that I am right smack in the "older age" stage of life, I know my life will come to an end sooner rather than later. When God sends for me, though, I know I'll have a home in heaven with a warm, welcoming light in the window.

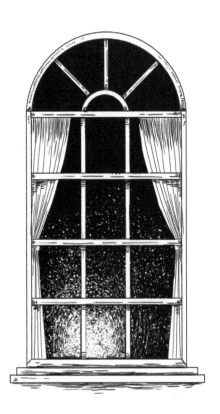

PART THREE

CELEBRATING THE GIFTS OF THE PAST

The Four Chaplains

Valor is a gift. Those having it never know for
sure they have it until the test comes.

Carl Sandburg

Floating helplessly in the freezing waters, First Sergeant Michael Warish accepted his fate, fully aware that life expectancy in these cold waters was about twenty minutes. Surrounded by hundreds of his equally doomed shipmates, he saw the blinking red lights of their life preservers and thought of Christmas lights.

Only minutes before, Michael, along with 902 officers, servicemen, and civilian workers, had been aboard the *SS Dorchester*. This United States Army Transport had left New York Harbor on January 23, 1943, bound for an Army base in Greenland. Joined in Newfoundland by two other freighters and three US Coast Guard Cutters, the convoy headed across a stretch of sea referred to as Torpedo Junction. Although freezing temperatures caused ice to form on the ships and slowed down the convoy, it finally was only 150 miles from Greenland.

Daylight would bring air protection from the American base, but until then, those aboard the *Dorchester* were well aware of the danger facing them. They knew the Germans had been ordered to hunt down the convoy. Four Army chaplains circulated among the frightened young men, some lying wide-eyed in their bunks, others playing cards or nervously making "small talk." Those chaplains were Lt. George L. Fox, Lt.

Alexander D. Goode, Lt. John P. Washington, and Lt. Clark V. Poling. These four chaplains calmed fears and eased tensions any way they could: for example, passing out soda crackers to alleviate seasickness caused by the stormy sea.

The worst fear of those aboard the *Dorchester* was realized. The Germans were successful in their mission. When only one thousand yards from the *Dorchester,* they fired three torpedoes, one of which ripped into the *Dorchester* seventy seconds later. The initial explosion killed dozens outright, and a wave of cold water entering the ship quickly drowned dozens more. The lights went out, steam pipes split, and bunks collapsed like cards atop one another. The sounds of screaming and smell of gunpowder and ammonia filled the air as panicked men struggled to get through dark and mangled passageways. Nearly one-third of those aboard died in the first moments of the disaster.

Michael Warish and other eyewitnesses saw the four chaplains remain calm during the horror following the attacks that early morning of February 3, 1943. The chaplains seemed to be everywhere, helping in whatever way they could until the very end. The chaplains first distributed life preservers and assisted others to abandon the ship. For those who wanted it, the chaplains prayed with them, and for those requesting it, Father Washington gave them absolution as they jumped over the side.

When the supplies ran out, the four chaplains gave up their own life preservers and their gloves. One soldier, Walter Miller, saw men in seemingly catatonic states bunched against the railings of the ship. Too afraid to jump into the freezing, swirling sea, they awaited the inevitability of being swallowed by it. Over the noise, he heard a terror-filled voice repeating, "I can't find my life jacket." Turning toward that voice, Miller heard Chaplain Fox say, "Here's one, soldier." Then Miller witnessed Fox remove his life jacket and put it on the soldier. Similarly, the other chaplains gave their life jackets to soldiers.

The four chaplains courageously offered a tenuous chance of survival to others with the full knowledge of the consequences to themselves. In the eighteen minutes it took the *Dorchester* to sink, the four chaplains insisted soldiers use the places on the limited number of lifeboats. Michael Warish and other rescued soldiers witnessed the four unwavering chaplains—a Catholic, a Jew, and two Protestants—standing on the deck, locking arms and praying in unison as the *Dorchester* slipped below the surface of the deep icy water of the North Atlantic.

Every Christmas until he died in 2003, Michael thought about the red lights of the life preservers reminding him of Christmas as he faced death in the freezing water thousands of miles from home. Even more, the willing service and sacrifice of the four valiant chaplains reminded him of what Christmas is all about: love, faith, and giving.

The four chaplains gave the ultimate gift for the soldiers, their country, and the God they served. They gave their lives so that others could enjoy the gift of life—and Christmas.

> *Note: Although the four chaplains (along with seven hundred others) died in a cold watery grave, their courage in the face of great danger has warmed the hearts of thousands around the world for generations. These brave men have received numerous awards posthumously, just to mention a few:*
>
> *The Purple Heart*
> *The Distinguished Service Cross*
>
> *The Four Chaplains Medal, a decoration approved by an Act of Congress on July 14, 1960, recognizing the extraordinary heroism displayed by them when they sacrificed*

their lives by giving up their life preservers to other men aboard the sinking SS Dorchester during World War II.

For more information, visit www.fourchaplains.org.

Silent Night

Music is well said to be the speech of angels.

Thomas Carlyle

"Silent Night," one of the best-loved Christmas songs ever, has been translated into more than forty-four languages, and people sing it on every continent. More than three hundred artists have recorded it; particularly popular were Bing Crosby, Elvis Presley, Mahalia Jackson (sung in English), Enya (sung in Irish), Andrea Bocelli (sung in Italian), and other notable musicians such as Susan Boyle (sung in English), whose version was a hit worldwide in 2009.

"Silent Night" is known as "The Carol That Stopped a War," for troops sang it together in French, English, and German during the Christmas truce of 1914 as it was one of the few carols that soldiers on both sides of the front line knew. The singing of Silent Night magically neutralized all hostilities on both sides for Christmas Day and in some areas until New Year's Day.

In contrast to the fame this song has enjoyed, its origin is quite humble. Romantic stories and legends add their own details to the known facts, according to the Silent Night Society. However, historians agree that Joseph Mohr wrote the words in 1816. With simple phrases in six short stanzas, he retold the story of Christ's birth.

Historians also agree that the song was first performed in 1818 on a guitar in the small Church of St. Nicholas, in the tiny village of Oberndorf, Austria. Joseph Mohr, Curate of the church, loved music and, to the delight of his parishioners, frequently played the guitar in addition to preaching during the worship services.

The young pastor believed music was particularly important for the Christmas service, but the church's badly damaged organ seemed beyond repair. Some historians speculated that Mohr overestimated the damage because he wanted to use his guitar for the Christmas service. With his musical background, he also knew that the traditional Christmas carols would not sound right on a stringed instrument. For the music, Mohr asked Franz Grüber, a friend and a more skilled composer than he was, if he could compose music to be accompanied by guitar in time for that evening's midnight Mass. Impressed by the beautiful lyrics Mohr had written, Grüber immediately began to work on the musical composition.

At midnight, parishioners filled St. Nicholas Church, expecting to hear the organist playing resounding notes of Christmas music. Instead, their church building was silent. Mohr explained the organ was broken but that new music would be played for the midnight Mass. With Mohr strumming the guitar, he and Grüber sang with the choir, joining in four-part harmony. Father Mohr proceeded with the evening celebration. Even without their organ, parishioners felt they had experienced a unique and memorable Christmas Eve service.

The story of "Silent Night" almost ended that evening as Mohr put the music away with no thoughts of using it again. However, an organ repairman found the manuscript in 1825 and revived the carol. Although it was causing an enormous stir across Europe, Grüber and Mohr remained unaware of the accolades their music was creating. Penniless, Father Mohr died of pneumonia in 1848 at the age of fifty-five. He never learned his song was spreading around the world.

Grüber first heard of the carol's success in 1854 when the concertmaster for King Frederick William IV of Prussia began searching for its authors. When word reached Grüber, then sixty-seven, he sent a letter to Berlin telling the origins of the song. When Grüber died in 1863, his authorship was still challenged. However, historians later confirmed that Grüber and Mohr were indeed the authors. Today, the lyrics and melody are in the public domain.

Even those who know nothing of its captivating history join legions of others who for two hundred years have felt joy and peace when they sing or hear the beautiful words and music of "Silent Night":

Silent night! Holy Night! All is calm, all is bright.
Round yon virgin mother and child!
Holy Infant, so tender and mild,
Sleep in heavenly peace.
Sleep in heavenly peace.
Silent night! Holy night! Shepherds quake at the sight!
Glories stream from Heaven afar,
Heav'nly hosts sing Alleluia, Christ, the Saviour, is born!
Christ, the Saviour, is born!
Silent Night! Holy night! Son of God, love's pure light.
Radiant beams from Thy holy face,
With the dawn of redeeming grace, Jesus, Lord, at Thy birth,
Jesus, Lord, at Thy birth.

Music and Lyrics:
Joseph Möhr and Franz Grüber

The Carol That Stopped a War

Let us therefore make every effort
to do what leads to peace.

Romans 14:19 (NIV)

"Silent Night," one of the world's favorite Christmas carols, played an intriguing role in the legendary Christmas Truce of 1914. In July of 1914, Pope Benedict XV called for a truce on the first Christmas after World War I started, but his appeal was officially rejected. Remarkably an impromptu truce was initiated by two-thirds of the troops—more than one hundred thousand British, Belgian, and French soldiers put down their rifles, stepped out of their trenches, and engaged in friendly visiting with their German enemies.

It is unclear what motivated the troops to initiate the truce on their own. One account said the power of the carol "Silent Night" was never so clear as on Christmas Eve when fighting on the battlefields stopped, and a lone soldier's exquisite voice made history. The author of *Silent Night: The Story of the World War I Christmas Truce*, Stanley Weintraub, said it started with German officer Walter Kirchhoff, a tenor with the Berlin Opera. The song made a memorable impact on many of the soldiers, including Private Albert Moren of the Second Queen's Regiment, who said, "It was a beautiful moonlight night, frost on the ground, white almost everywhere, and …there was a lot of commotion…and then there were those lights … And they sang 'Silent Night'—'Stille Nacht.' I shall never forget it. It was one of the highlights of my life."[7]

Another account describes how on Christmas Eve, German soldiers began lighting candles, putting them on small trees, and lifting them up to be seen at a distance. British sentries reported the appearance of small lights, and within moments of that sighting, the British began hearing a few Germans soldiers singing a Christmas carol. Along the German line, other soldiers joined in, harmonizing. The words heard were "Stille Nacht, Heilige Nacht," but the British soldiers recognized the melody as "Silent night, holy night" and began singing in English along with the Germans.

A British soldier, Graham Williams, was on guard in a forward trench. "I was standing on the firestep gazing towards the German lines and thinking what a different sort of Christmas Eve this was from any I had experienced in the past."[8] Williams and the men in his company watched as more lighted trees appeared along the enemy's battle line. As the singing continued on both sides, Williams remembered saying, "Well, this was really a most extraordinary thing—two nations both singing the same carol in the middle of a war."[9]

The next morning, in some places, German soldiers emerged from their trenches, calling out "Merry Christmas" in English. Allied soldiers came out warily to greet them. In other locations, Germans held up signs reading, "You no shoot, we no shoot."[10] Over the course of the day, troops exchanged gifts of cigarettes, food, and other small items and showed each other family pictures. One high-ranking officer wrote in a memo that if troops were allowed to socialize, they would develop a "live and let live" theory of life, and there would be no wars. Frank Richards, an eyewitness of the unofficial truce, wrote in his wartime diary that some German soldiers spoke perfect English, with one saying how fed up he was with the war and how he would be glad when it was all over. His British counterpart agreed. Once again, the power of singing "Silent Night" together!

While the truce was widespread, it was not universal. Evidence suggests that in many places, firing continued, and, of course, it was only a truce, not peace. At least it allowed both sides to finally bury their dead comrades, whose bodies had lain for weeks on "no man's land" between the opposing trenches. Hostilities returned, in some places later on Christmas Day and in others not until after New Year's Day. "I remember the silence, the eerie sound of silence," one soldier from the Fifth Battalion later recalled to *The Observer*. "It was a short peace in a terrible war."

The truce ended just as it had begun, by mutual agreement, and as one eyewitness said, after a truly "silent night." In the one hundred plus years since the truce, the legendary event has been considered as a kind of miracle, a rare moment of peace just a few months into a war that would eventually claim over 15 million lives. Although World War I was definitely a dark hour of history, it had significant results affecting world governance. Still, a century later, the truce has been remembered as a testament to the power of hope and humanity. The fact that the Christmas Truce of 1914 remains so widely commemorated is a reminder that at the heart of people everywhere is a deep human desire for peace, no matter how fleeting. As we celebrate the birth of Jesus, let us remember He truly is the Prince of Peace promised in Isaiah 9:6 (NIV):

For to us a child is born, to us a son is given, and the government will be on his shoulders. And he will be called Wonderful Counselor, Mighty God, Everlasting Father, Prince of Peace.

I Heard the Bells on Christmas Day

Let us have music for Christmas…
Sound the trumpet of joy and rebirth;
Let each of us try, with a song in our hearts,
To bring peace to men on earth.

Mildred L. Jarrell

When in a high school literature class, I read "Christmas Bells," a poem Henry Wadsworth Longfellow wrote in 1863. His wife had died tragically in a fire, the Civil War was raging, and his son had been seriously wounded in the war. Upon hearing the bells on Christmas day, the poet told of his despair that "hate is strong and mocks the song of peace on earth, good-will to men." In contrast, he concluded his poem with the bells carrying renewed hope, using the refrain "peace on earth, good-will to men," a reference to the King James Version of Luke 2:14.

Bing Crosby recorded verses one, two, six, and seven in 1956 and named the song "I Heard the Bells on Christmas Day." The song became a top hit, and other versions were recorded by various musicians, including Johnny Cash, Harry Belafonte, Andy Williams, and Casting Crowns. Capturing Henry Wadsworth Longfellow's message in his poem, the song continues to be one of Christmas's most beautiful carols, bringing a timely message of hope, peace, and joy every Christmas season.

"Christmas Bells"

I heard the bells on Christmas Day
Their old, familiar carols play,
And wild and sweet
The words repeat
Of peace on earth, good-will to men!

And thought how, as the day had come,
The belfries of all Christendom
Had rolled along
The unbroken song
Of peace on earth, good-will to men!

Till ringing, singing on its way,
The world revolved from night to day,
A voice, a chime,
A chant sublime
Of peace on earth, good-will to men!

Then from each black, accursed mouth
The cannon thundered in the South,
And with the sound
The carols drowned
Of peace on earth, good-will to men!

It was as if an earthquake rent
The hearth-stones of a continent,
And made forlorn
The households born
Of peace on earth, good-will to men!

And in despair I bowed my head;
"There is no peace on earth," I said;

THE GIFTS OF CHRISTMAS

"For hate is strong,
And mocks the song
Of peace on earth, good-will to men!"
Then pealed the bells more loud and deep:
"God is not dead, nor doth He sleep;
The Wrong shall fail,
The Right prevail,
With peace on earth, good-will to men."
—Henry Wadsworth Longfellow

The Tablecloth

You are the God who performs miracles.

Psalm 77:14 (NIV)

"Christmas is only two days away!" cried the young pastor's panicked wife. She and her husband had worked hard to get an old and badly neglected church ready for its first service under their care. They had high hopes for a beautiful Christmas Eve service. When they almost had the church ready, a terrible rainstorm tore through the area. Rain poured onto the roof, causing a large area of plaster to fall off the wall behind the pulpit. This was the worst possible place for damage, for everybody in the church service would be looking right at it.

With heavy hearts and exhaustion from cleaning up the mess, the young couple headed home. Along the way, they saw a flea market where an auction was being held. The couple stopped to watch just as a beautifully handmade, ivory-colored, and ornately stitched tablecloth was held up for auction. The young pastor turned to his wife and exclaimed, "Don't you think this beautiful tablecloth is just the right size to cover up that awful hole behind the pulpit?" Fortunately, no one else was interested in the cloth, so they bought it and headed back to the church.

By this time, large snowflakes had begun to fall, and the temperature had plummeted. As they approached the church, they noticed an older woman shivering from the cold as she waited for a bus. The young couple was familiar with the bus schedule and knew another bus would not be stopping for nearly an hour, so they invited her to wait inside the church where she would be warm. She gratefully accepted their invitation and sat down on a pew.

Meanwhile, the pastor got out a ladder so he and his wife could see if the tablecloth would camouflage the terribly damaged wall behind the pulpit. The young couple stood in awe—they could hardly believe their eyes! The cloth looked even more beautiful once it was spread out and hung up.

Gripping the edges of the pews as she hurried down the aisle, the older woman broke the silence. "Reverend," she asked. "Where did you get that tapestry?" Before he could answer, she asked him to check the lower right corner to see if the initials EBG were stitched there. They were. "Those are my initials!" the woman gasped. She had made this tablecloth thirty-five years ago and could hardly believe how the pastor had acquired the tablecloth. She explained that before the war, she and her husband lived in Austria. When the Nazis came in, her husband insisted she leave. He planned to follow her the next week. He never made it out of the country and was imprisoned. She was told he was dead and never saw her husband or her home again.

The pastor wanted to give her the tablecloth, but she was adamant he keep it for the church. The pastor insisted on driving her home, for she lived on the other side of the city.

What a wonderful Christmas Eve service they had. Many from the neighborhood came to it. The Christmas songs and hymns and the pastor's inspirational words of the Christmas story touched the hearts of young and old alike. The Christmas spirit was warm and rekindled a new feeling of caring and community among the people. At the end of the service, the pastor and his wife thanked each person at the door for attending, and many said they would return.

Although everyone else had left, one older man remained. The pastor had hired him to do some painting, and he had come to the service at the pastor's invitation. He continued to sit in one of the pews and stare. The pastor wondered why he wasn't leaving. The man asked him where he got the hanging on the front wall because it was identical to a tablecloth that his wife had made years ago when they lived in Austria before the war.

"How could there be two so much alike?" he asked. He told the pastor how when the Nazis came, he insisted his wife flee the country for her safety. His plan was to follow her a week later, but he was arrested and put in a camp. He never saw his wife or his home again. The pastor told the distraught man he might be able to help him find his wife. He told the man about the woman who had been at the church very recently. "Can it be," gasped the old man, tears streaming down his cheeks, "that she is alive?"

The young pastor and his wife drove the old man to the home where they had taken the woman earlier. He helped the man climb the stairs to the woman's apartment, knocked on the door, and waited. When she came to the door, she immediately recognized her husband. They embraced and cried, and embraced and cried some more. The young pastor and his wife saw the greatest reunion they could ever imagine. It was truly a Christmas miracle!

Postscript:

"This story was originally called "The Gold and Ivory Tablecloth" and was written by the Reverend Howard C. Schade, pastor of the First Reformed Church in Nyack, New York. It was published in the December 1954 issue of Reader's Digest, anthologized in

Alice Gray's Christmas Stories for the Heart in 1998, and appeared in various other versions, including those on the internet. Since the story is undated, there is no way of telling how long the separated couple reunited by the tablecloth had been apart.

"As for verifying the truth of this remarkable story, there is little to go on. Its author passed away in 1989. Regardless of the unknowns, it is an amazing story of what some might call "coincidences:" the plaster, the auction, the bus stop, the handyman job. To those of us who believe in miracles, these were not mere coincidences. They were threads purposefully woven by a loving God into a beautiful tapestry, and ultimately, a Christmas miracle."

The foregoing Postscript is quoted from the Snopes website.[11]

The Gift of the Magi

> It's not how much we give but how
> much love we put into giving.
>
> *Mother Teresa*

The intriguing twists and turns in the life of O. Henry, the American author of "The Gift of the Magi," clearly inspired a rich legacy of literature. The title of perhaps O. Henry's most famous story refers to the three "wise men," or magi, who brought precious gifts to the child Jesus. First published in 1905, "The Gift of the Magi" continues to be a favorite Christmas story among readers the world over.

One dollar and eighty-seven cents. That was all. And sixty cents of it was in pennies. Pennies saved one and two at a time by bulldozing the grocer and the vegetable man and the butcher until one's cheeks burned with the silent imputation of parsimony that such close dealing implied. Three times Della counted it. One dollar and eighty-seven cents. And the next day would be Christmas.

There was clearly nothing left to do but flop down on the shabby little couch and howl. So Della did it. Which instigates the moral reflection that life is made up of sobs, sniffles, and smiles, with sniffles predominating.

While the mistress of the home is gradually subsiding from the first stage to the second, take a look at the home. A furnished flat at $8 per week. It did not exactly beggar description, but it certainly had that word on the look-out for the mendicancy squad.

In the vestibule below was a letter-box into which no letter would go, and an electric button from which no mortal finger could coax a ring. Also appertaining thereunto was a card bearing the name "Mr. James Dillingham Young."

The "Dillingham" had been flung to the breeze during a former period of prosperity when its possessor was being paid $30 per week. Now, when the income was shrunk to $20, the letters of "Dillingham" looked blurred, as though they were thinking seriously of contracting to a modest and unassuming D. But whenever Mr. James Dillingham Young came home and reached his flat above he was called "Jim" and greatly hugged by Mrs. James Dillingham Young, already introduced to you as Della. Which is all very good.

Della finished her cry and attended to her cheeks with the powder rag. She stood by the window and looked out dully at a grey cat walking a grey fence in a grey backyard. To-morrow would be Christmas Day, and she had only $1.87 with which to buy Jim a present. She had been saving every penny she could for months, with this result. Twenty dollars a week doesn't go far. Expenses had been greater than she had calculated. They always are. Only $1.87 to buy a present for Jim. Her Jim. Many a happy hour she had spent planning for something nice for him. Something fine and rare and sterling—something just a little bit near to being worthy of the honour of being owned by Jim.

There was a pier-glass between the windows of the room. Perhaps you have seen a pier-glass in an $8 flat. A very thin and very agile person may, by observing his reflection in a rapid sequence of longitudinal strips, obtain a fairly accurate conception of his looks. Della, being slender, had mastered the art.

Suddenly she whirled from the window and stood before the glass. Her eyes were shining brilliantly, but her face had lost its colour within twenty seconds. Rapidly she pulled down her hair and let it fall to its full length.

Now, there were two possessions of the James Dillingham Youngs in which they both took a mighty pride. One was Jim's gold watch that had been his father's and his grandfather's. The other was Della's hair. Had the Queen of Sheba lived in the flat across the airshaft, Della would have let her hair hang out of the window some day to dry just to depreciate Her Majesty's jewels and gifts. Had King Solomon been the janitor, with all his treasures piled up in the basement, Jim would have pulled out his watch every time he passed, just to see him pluck at his beard from envy.

So now Della's beautiful hair fell about her, rippling and shining like a cascade of brown waters. It reached below her knee and made itself almost a garment for her. And then she did it up again nervously and quickly. Once she faltered for a minute and stood still while a tear or two splashed on the worn red carpet.

On went her old brown jacket; on went her old brown hat. With a whirl of skirts and with the brilliant sparkle still in her eyes, she fluttered out of the door and down the stairs to the street.

Where she stopped the sign read: "Mme Sofronie. Hair Goods of All Kinds." One flight up Della ran, and collected herself, panting. Madame, large, too white, chilly, hardly looked the "Sofronie."

"Will you buy my hair?" asked Della.

"I buy hair," said Madame. "Take yer hat off and let's have a sight at the looks of it."

Down rippled the brown cascade.

"Twenty dollars," said Madame, lifting the mass with a practised hand.

"Give it to me quick" said Della.

Oh, and the next two hours tripped by on rosy wings. Forget the hashed metaphor. She was ransacking the stores for Jim's present.

She found it at last. It surely had been made for Jim and no one else. There was no other like it in any of the stores, and she had turned all of them inside out. It was a platinum fob chain simple and chaste in design, properly proclaiming its value by substance alone and not by meretricious ornamentation—as all good things should do. It was even worthy of The Watch. As soon as she saw it she knew that it must be Jim's. It was like him. Quietness and value—the description applied to both. Twenty-one dollars they took from her for it, and she hurried home with the 78 cents. With that chain on his watch Jim might be properly anxious about the time in any company. Grand as the watch was, he sometimes looked at it on the sly on account of the old leather strap that he used in place of a chain.

When Della reached home her intoxication gave way a little to prudence and reason. She got out her curling irons and lighted the gas and went to work repairing the ravages made by generosity added to love. Which is always a tremendous task dear friends—a mammoth task.

Within forty minutes her head was covered with tiny, close-lying curls that made her look wonderfully like a truant schoolboy. She looked at her reflection in the mirror long, carefully, and critically.

"If Jim doesn't kill me," she said to herself, "before he takes a second look at me, he'll say I look like a Coney Island chorus girl. But what could I do—oh! what could I do with a dollar and eighty-seven cents?"

At 7 o'clock the coffee was made and the frying-pan was on the back of the stove hot and ready to cook the chops.

Jim was never late. Della doubled the fob chain in her hand and sat on the corner of the table near the door that he always entered. Then she heard his step on the stair away down on the first flight, and she turned white for just a moment. She had a habit of saying little silent prayers about the simplest everyday things, and now she whispered: "Please, God, make him think I am still pretty."

The door opened and Jim stepped in and closed it. He looked thin and very serious. Poor fellow, he was only twenty-two—and to be burdened with a family! He needed a new overcoat and he was without gloves.

Jim stepped inside the door, as immovable as a setter at the scent of quail. His eyes were fixed upon Della, and there was an expression in them that she could not read, and it terrified her. It was not anger, nor surprise, nor disapproval, nor horror, nor any of the sentiments that she had been prepared for. He simply stared at her fixedly with that peculiar expression on his face.

Della wriggled off the table and went for him.

"Jim, darling," she cried, "don't look at me that way. I had my hair cut off and sold it because I couldn't have lived through Christmas without giving you a present. It'll grow out again—you won't mind, will you? I just had to do it. My hair grows awfully fast. Say 'Merry Christmas!' Jim, and let's be happy. You don't know what a nice—what a beautiful, nice gift I've got for you."

"You've cut off your hair?" asked Jim, laboriously, as if he had not arrived at that patent fact yet, even after the hardest mental labour.

"Cut it off and sold it," said Della. "Don't you like me just as well, anyhow? I'm me without my hair, ain't I?"

Jim looked about the room curiously.

"You say your hair is gone?" he said, with an air almost of idiocy.

"You needn't look for it," said Della. "It's sold, I tell you—sold and gone, too. It's Christmas Eve, boy. Be good to me, for it went for you. Maybe the hairs of my head were numbered," she went on with a sudden serious sweetness, "but nobody could ever count my love for you. Shall I put the chops on, Jim?"

Out of his trance Jim seemed quickly to wake. He enfolded his Della. For ten seconds let us regard with discreet scrutiny some inconsequential object in the other direction. Eight dollars a week or a million a year—what is the difference? A mathematician or a wit would give you the wrong answer. The magi brought valuable gifts, but that was not among them. This dark assertion will be illuminated later on.

Jim drew a package from his overcoat pocket and threw it upon the table.

"Don't make any mistake, Dell," he said, "about me. I don't think there's anything in the way of a haircut or a shave or a shampoo that could make me like my girl any less. But if you'll unwrap that package you may see why you had me going a while at first."

White fingers and nimble tore at the string and paper. And then an ecstatic scream of joy; and then, alas! a quick feminine change to hysterical tears and wails, necessitating the immediate employment of all the comforting powers of the lord of the flat.

For there lay The Combs—the set of combs, side and back, that Della had worshipped long in a Broadway window. Beautiful combs, pure tortoise-shell, with jewelled rims—just the shade to wear in the beautiful vanished hair. They were expensive combs, she knew, and her heart had simply craved and yearned over them without the least hope of possession. And now, they were hers, but the tresses that should have adorned the coveted adornments were gone.

But she hugged them to her bosom, and at length she was able to look up with dim eyes and a smile and say: "My hair grows so fast, Jim!"

And then Della leaped up like a little singed cat and cried, "Oh, oh!"

Jim had not yet seen his beautiful present. She held it out to him eagerly upon her open palm. The dull precious metal seemed to flash with a reflection of her bright and ardent spirit.

"Isn't it a dandy, Jim? I hunted all over town to find it. You'll have to look at the time a hundred times a day now. Give me your watch. I want to see how it looks on it."

Instead of obeying, Jim tumbled down on the couch and put his hands under the back of his head and smiled.

"Dell," said he, "let's put our Christmas presents away and keep 'em a while. They're too nice to use just at present. I sold the watch to get the money to buy your combs. And now suppose you put the chops on."

The magi, as you know, were wise men—wonderfully wise men—who brought gifts to the Babe in the manger. They invented the art of giving Christmas presents. Being wise, their gifts were no doubt wise ones, possibly bearing the privilege of exchange in case of duplication. And here I have lamely related to you the uneventful chronicle of two foolish children in a flat who most unwisely sacrificed for each other the greatest treasures of their house. But in a last word to the wise of these days let it be said that of all who give gifts these two were the wisest. Of all who give and receive gifts, such as they are wisest. Everywhere they are wisest. They are the magi.[12]

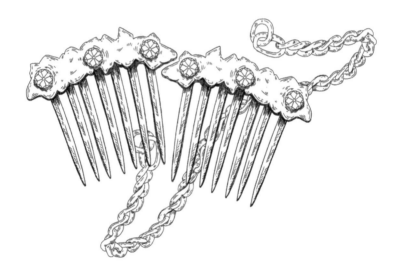

Wartime Christmas

> Our God is the God of the unexpected. A few
> things could be more unexpected than the
> King of heaven being born in a stable.
>
> *Bill Crowder*

Are the necessary ingredients for the celebration of Christmas a tree, toys, gifts, turkey, family, and friends? No, none of these is really essential. This was revealed to me during World War II in a foreign country, and the lesson has lasted a lifetime.

It was the Christmas of 1944. My Fourth Infantry Division had just been relieved by a fresh division after a bruising and bloody battle in the Hurtgen Forest. After having been on the battle line for 188 consecutive days, we had been redeployed to what was supposed to be a static front in Luxemburg to gain a much-needed rest, clean and repair our weapons, and rebuild a division from one-third to full strength.

After three days of the all-quiet on the sector of our front, there came the mad rush of the frantic and feverish efforts called The Battle of the Bulge. Our weakened and weary troops were hit hard with a ceaseless artillery barrage. Two companies of my battalion were quickly overrun and captured.

Although outmaneuvered and with half of our weapons in the ordnance depot, we fought back with all the fury we could muster. After three days of battle, the order came down that we were to hold our position at all costs.

It was late Christmas Eve, and there had been a lull in the fighting because the enemy was regrouping for a new offensive. To stand our ground would be a miracle. Then, to our utter surprise, battle-ready reinforcements in full strength moved in to occupy our position. We gathered our gear, climbed about our G.I. trucks, and started moving back to the rear echelon.

The men on my truck were strangely silent. Even though we were relieved to be leaving the front, something was wrong. It was Christmas Eve, we were thousands of miles from home, and all the past memories of the yuletide season were like a dream.

The journey seemed to be endless. At last, as we were winding down a mountainside, the village below became clearly visible in the moonlight. Our hearts were cheered by the prospects of sleeping in a bed or at least a dry room.

As we approached the village, it was evident that the enemy had not only been there but was still there. Not a single unoccupied billet was left. New depths of despair emerged, for it appeared that the snow would be our mattress this Christmas.

We tried farmhouses, but these too were filled. Finally, my platoon secured a barn. Sleeping bags were unfolded, and soon complete hush prevailed.

With straw for my pillow, I felt I could dream of only a miserable Christmas. The words of Longfellow described my feelings:

And in despair I bowed my head,
"There is no peace on earth," I said,
"For hate is strong and mocks the song
of peace on earth, good-will to men."

Then, suddenly, it hit me. Nearly two thousand years ago, there was no room in the inn. Jesus was ushered into the world, and his first abode was a shabby stable. As I nestled down to sleep in the hay, I realized the wonder of God's Son doing the same.

What a Christmas! My heart sprang to life as I pondered the wonder of it all. Christmas is not so much a sparkling feeling or a season of excess but an earthy, simple reality. In that moment, the nearness of God was very real.

Every year since, the Christmas story has carried a more serious reality and significance to me. From that terrible war, I brought home a lesson I will never forget. While the whole world seems to be caught up in the bright lights and festive carols, I am sobered by the thought of the lowly Christmas shelter my fellow soldiers and I found in the forlorn, battle-scarred countryside. It wasn't much different from the stable Jesus slept in on his first night on this earth. It was in the midst of a world full of hostility, war, and hate that

Hope was born.

James F. Cole

A Thousand Winds That Blow

Do not stand at my grave and weep,
I am not there; I do not sleep.
I am a thousand winds that blow,
I am the diamond glints on snow,
I am the sun on ripened grain,
I am the gentle autumn rain.
When you awaken in the morning's hush
I am the swift uplifting rush
Of quiet birds in circling flight.
I am the soft starlight at night.
Do not stand at my grave and cry,
I am not there; I did not die.

Mary Elizabeth Frye

My brother Phill was born on Christmas Eve. Because he loved to read, a book was usually my birthday gift to him. He, in turn, gave me books or clippings or copies of something he thought I would enjoy or find interesting. One year, he gave me a copy of one of his favorite poems, "A Thousand Winds That Blow," or sometimes called "Do Not Stand at My Grave and Weep." In a hand-written note, Phill explained that this poem's author was orphaned when she was three. Phill underlined the rest of the note to me:

the same age I was when our father was killed.

Vietnam was one of Phill's duty stations during his Navy career. This gave him empathy for those killed in battle and a special "connection" to this poem. Phill had become aware of this poem when he heard about a young soldier who had been killed in Northern Ireland by a bomb, and his father had read this poem at his memorial service.

After a brief, agonizing battle with pancreatic cancer, Phill died. My emotions hit rock bottom from losing my much-loved brother and life-long friend. A military memorial service celebrated his life and his twenty years of service in the Navy. As part of the service, I was honored to read Phill's favorite poem. This poem was never copyrighted, and my curious brother had wondered why. He shared the author's explanation: "It belongs to the world; it didn't belong to me. It was written out of love—for comfort."

The author's wish came true. Every Christmas Eve, on Phill's birthday, I read this poem, and my heart is made lighter:

> Do not stand at my grave and weep,
> I am not there; I do not sleep.
> [...]
> Do not stand at my grave and cry,
> I am not there; I did not die.
>
> —Mary Elizabeth Frye

Looking Back

> When we recall Christmas past, we usually find
> that the simplest things—not the great occasions—
> give off the greatest glow of happiness.
>
> *Bob Hope*

When I reflect on my life and the joy of giving and receiving gifts during the Christmas season, I am reminded of Edgar A. Guest's poem "Looking Back." This English-born American writer does not refer specifically to Christmas, but the essence of his message beautifully captures the true meaning of the season.

"Looking Back"

I might have been rich if I'd wanted the gold instead of
  the friendships I've made.
I might have had fame if I'd sought for renown in the
  hours when I purposely played.
Now I'm standing today on the far edge of life, and I'm
  just looking backward to see
What I've done with the years and the days that were
  mine, and all that has happened to me.
I haven't built much of a fortune to leave to those who
  shall carry my name,
And nothing I've done shall entitle me now to a place on
  the tablets of fame.

But I've loved the great sky and its spaces of blue; I've
    lived with the birds and the trees;
I've turned from the splendor of silver and gold to share
    in such pleasures as these.
I've given my time to the children who came, together
    we've romped and we've played.
And I wouldn't exchange the glad hours spent with them
    for the money that I might have made.
I chose to be known and be loved by the few, and was deaf
    to the plaudits of men;
And I'd make the same choice should the chance come to
    me to live my life over again.
I've lived with my friends and I've share in their joys,
    known sorrow with all of its tears;
I've harvested much from my acres of life, though some
    say I've squandered my years.
For much that is fine has been mine to enjoy, and I think
    I have lived to my best,
And I have no regret, as I'm nearing the end, for the gold
    that I might have possessed.

—Edgar A. Guest, 1959

PART FOUR

CELEBRATING THE GIFT OF FAITH FOR THE FUTURE

While the holiday season is arguably the happiest time of the year, it can also be one of the most overwhelming. Family conflicts, political strife, and even a global pandemic can impact the way many celebrate Christmas, Hanukkah, and other holidays from year to year. For those who have lost a loved one, the Christmas season may be terribly painful. For Christians, focusing on the reason for the season, the birth of Jesus Christ, can help bring a sense of calm to a stressful and, at times, disappointing season. There are more than a few Bible verses and other writings that can help you find joy, gratefulness, and perspective this holiday season and those in the future.

May the following scriptures, quotes, poems, and prayers be a gift of faith to you this Christmas.

Quotable Christmas

Celebrating the Gifts of Love and Joy

When our attention is turned only to the parties
and presents, it becomes too easy to forget Christ
at Christmas. Let us not forget the best and most
wonderful Gift that God has given to us—Jesus.

Mother Teresa[13]

God goes to those who have time to hear him—and so
on this cloudless night he went to simple shepherds.

Max Lucado[14]

[This] is what Christmas is about; that is why we use bright
colors and sing joyful songs at Christmas—we want to
celebrate because we've got Somebody Who loves us.

Norman Vincent Peale[15]

Christmas is not a time nor a season, but a state of
mind. To cherish peace and goodwill, to be plenteous
in mercy, is to have the real spirit of Christmas.

President Calvin Coolidge[16]

I have always thought of Christmas…as a good time;
a kind, forgiving, charitable, pleasant time…when
men and women seem by one consent to open up
their shut-up hearts freely…and I say, God bless it!

Charles Dickens[17]

Christmas is a season for kindling the fire for hospitality
in the hall, the genial flame of charity in the heart.

Washington Irving[18]

A good Conscience is a continual Christmas.

Benjamin Franklin[19]

The best of all gifts around any Christmas tree is the
presence of a happy family all wrapped up in each other.

Burton Hills[20]

Christmas, my child, is love in action. Every time
we love, every time we give, it's Christmas.

Dale Evans[21]

And when the Lord Jesus has become your peace, remember,
there is another thing: good will towards men. Do not
try to keep Christmas without good will towards men.

Charles Spurgeon[22]

Dear sinner, you can never truly enjoy Christmas as I
enjoy it and as millions of others do, until you can look
up into the Father's face and tell Him that you have
received his Christmas gift, that you have the joy He
promised by the angels that first Christmas night!

John R. Rice[23]

Let us contemplate the child and let ourselves
be caught up in his tender love.

Pope Francis[24]

My idea of Christmas, whether old-fashioned or modern,
is very simple: loving others. Come to think of it,
why do we have to wait for Christmas to do that?

Bob Hope[25]

Celebrating the Gifts of Hope and Peace

God never gives someone a gift they are not capable of
receiving. If He gives us the gift of Christmas, it is because
we all have the ability to understand and receive it.

Pope Francis[26]

Peace on earth will come to stay, when
we live Christmas every day.

Helen Steiner Rice[27]

Christmas is a holiday that we celebrate not as
individuals nor as a nation, but as a human family.

President Ronald Reagan[28]

The only blind person at Christmas time is
he who has not Christmas in his heart.

Helen Keller[29]

Christmas means the beginning of Christianity—
and a second chance for the world.

Peter Marshall[30]

Mankind is a great, an immense family. This is proved
by what we feel in our hearts at Christmas.
Pope John XXIII[31]

It came without ribbons! It came without tags! It
came without packages, boxes, or bags! [...] Maybe
Christmas, he thought, doesn't come from a store.
Maybe Christmas, perhaps, means a little bit more!
Theodor Seuss Geisel (Dr. Seuss)[32]

Celebrating Gifts of the Past

This is Christmas-day, the anniversary of the world's
greatest event...that day holds time together.
Alexander Smith[33]

Christ was born in the first century, yet he belongs to all
centuries. He was born a Jew, yet He belongs to all races.
George W. Truett[34]

Our hearts grow tender with childhood memories and
love of kindred, and we are better throughout the year for
having, in spirit, become a child again at Christmastime.
Laura Ingalls Wilder[35]

Christmas is a season not only of rejoicing but of reflection.
Winston Churchill[36]

If everything special and warm and happy in my
formative years could have been consolidated into
one word, that would have been "Christmas."
Gloria Gaither[37]

Celebrating the Gift of Faith for the Future

The miracle of Christmas is not on
34th Street; it's in Bethlehem.

Rick Warren[38]

The very purpose of Christ's coming into the world was
that he might offer up his life as a sacrifice for the sins of
men. He came to die. This is the heart of Christmas.

Billy Graham[39]

Jesus came into the world, that He
might come into your heart.

David Jeremiah[40]

At Christmas, the heart goes home.

Marjorie Holmes[41]

What is Christmas? It is tenderness for the past,
courage for the present, hope for the future. It is a
fervent wish that every path may lead to peace.

Agnes M. Pharo[42]

Faith is salted and peppered through everything at Christmas.
And I love at least one night by the Christmas tree to sing
and feel the quiet holiness of that time that's set apart to
celebrate love, friendship, and God's gift of the Christ child.

Amy Grant[43]

Who can add to Christmas? The perfect motive is that God so loved the world. The perfect gift is that He gave His only Son. The only requirement is to believe in Him. The reward of faith is that you shall have everlasting life.

Corrie ten Boom[44]

Rhythms and Rhymes
for Christmastime

"At Christmas"

A man is at his finest
towards the finish of the year;
He is almost what he should be
when the Christmas season is here;
Then he's thinking more of others
than he's thought the months before,
And the laughter of his children
is a joy worth toiling for.
He is less a selfish creature than
at any other time;
When the Christmas spirit rules him
he comes close to the sublime.
When it's Christmas man is bigger
and is better in his part;
He is keener for the service
that is prompted by the heart.
All the petty thoughts and narrow
seem to vanish for awhile
And the true reward he's seeking
is the glory of a smile.
Then for others he is toiling and
somehow it seems to me
That at Christmas he is almost
what God wanted him to be.

If I had to paint a picture of a man
I think I'd wait
Till he'd fought his selfish battles
and had put aside his hate.
I'd not catch him at his labors
when his thoughts are all of self,
On the long days and the dreary
when he's striving for himself.
I'd not take him when he's sneering,
when he's scornful or depressed,
But I'd look for him at Christmas
when he's shining at his best.
Man is ever in a struggle
and he's oft misunderstood;
There are days the worst that's in him
is the master of the good,
But at Christmas kindness rules him
and he puts himself aside
And his petty hates are vanquished
and his heart is opened wide.
Oh, I don't know how to say it,
but somehow it seems to me
That at Christmas man is almost
what God sent him here to be.

Edgar Guest

"Christmas Gift Suggestions"

To your enemy, forgiveness.
To an opponent, tolerance.
To a friend, your heart.
To a customer, service.
To all, charity.
To every child, a good example.
To yourself, respect.

Oren Arnold

"Someone is Missing at Christmas"

Let this be a loving reminder
That someone is missing today.
Someone our hearts still hold on to,
As we travel along life's way,
Someone who made life so special,
For all those who gather here,
Someone who won't be forgotten,
But cherished from year to year.
And now as we pause to remember,
Let us all fondly recall,
How dearly each of us loved her,
And oh…how she loved us all!

Author Unknown

"What Do You Want for Christmas?"

So many of you asked us (since Christmas is drawing
        near),
"What do you want for Christmas? What can we give this
        year?
If we say, "We want nothing!" you buy something anyway,
So here's a list of what we'd like; believe now what we say:
Pajamas for a little child, food to feed the poor.
Blankets for a shelter, and we ask but little more—
Perform good deeds and let us know,
Or volunteer your time.
These last are worth a fortune,
And they needn't cost a dime.
We have too many things now, vases, candles, tapes and
        clocks.
We have our fill of garments, ties, underwear and socks.
Candy is too fattening, crossword books we've more than
        twenty.
We don't need trays or plates or cups,
And knickknacks we have plenty.
We've no walls to hang more pictures;
We have no books we've not yet read,
So please take what you'd spend on us;
And help the poor instead!
Just send a Christmas card to us and tell us what you've
        done;
We'll open them on Christmas Eve and read them one
        by one.
It won't cost as much for postage as a package sent would
        do,
You'll need no wrapping paper, ribbons, ink, or glue.

And we'll thank God you listened to what we had to say.
So we could be the instruments to help someone this
way.

Author Unknown,
published in the Washington Post in 2002[45]

Christmas Prayers

Our prayers may be awkward. Our attempts
may be feeble. But since the power of prayer is
in the one who hears it and not in the one who
says it, our prayers do make a difference.

Max Lucado

These widely circulated and well-known prayers offer peace,
comfort, and inspiration to those willing to pray them. May
these prayers strengthen your faith at Christmastime and
always.

"A Christmas Prayer"

May the forgiving spirit of Him
to whom we dedicate this season
prevail again on earth.
May hunger disappear
and terrorists cease
their senseless acts.
May people live in freedom,
worshiping as they see fit,
loving others.
May the sanctity of the home
be ever preserved.

May peace, everlasting peace,
reign supreme.

Soundings, Vol. 2, No. 12
Fr. Brian Cavanaugh, TOR

"Prayer of Mother Teresa"

Let us preach you,
Dear Jesus, without preaching…
Not by words but by our example…
By the casting force, the sympathetic influence
Of what we do, the evident fullness of
The love our hearts bear to you.
Amen.

"The Serenity Prayer"

God, grant me the Serenity
To accept the things I cannot change,
Courage to change the things I can,
And Wisdom to know the difference.
Living one day at a time,
Enjoying one moment at a time,
Accepting hardship as the pathway to peace.
Taking, as He did, this sinful world as it is,
Not as I would have it.
Trusting that He will make all things right
if I surrender to His will.
That I may be reasonably happy in this life,
And supremely happy with Him forever in the next.
Amen.

Reinhold Niebuhr

"Irish Blessings"

May the road rise up to meet you.
May the wind always be at your back.
May the sunshine warm upon your face,
and rains fall soft upon your fields.
And until we meet again,
May God hold you in the palm of His hand.

***

May there always be work for your hands to do.
May your purse always hold a coin or two.
May the sun always shine on your windowpane.
May a rainbow be certain to follow each rain.
May the hand of a friend always be near you.
May God fill your heart with gladness to cheer you.

"A Prayer"

We thank you for this place in which we dwell,
for the love that unites us,
for the peace accorded us this day,
for the hope with which we expect the morrow,
for the work, the health, the food
and bright skies which make our lives
delightful for our friends in all parts of the earth.

Robert Louis Stevenson

"The Lord's Prayer"

Our Father in heaven,
hallowed be your name,
your kingdom come,
your will be done,
on earth as it is in heaven.
Give us today our daily bread.
And forgive us our debts,
as we also have forgiven our debtors.
And lead us not into temptation,
But deliver us from the evil one.

Matthew 6:9-13 (NIV)

"A Prayer for Peace"

On this Christmas, may we, the people of every race,
Nation, and religion, learn to love one another and
To forgive and be forgiven.
Then, the peace of Christ will prevail.

Coretta Scott King

Scriptures for the Season

For to us a child is born,
to us a son is given,
and the government will be on his shoulders.
And he will be called
Wonderful Counselor, Mighty God,
Everlasting Father, Prince of Peace.
Isaiah 9:6 (NIV)

Nothing is impossible for God.
Luke 1:37 (NLT)

In the same way, let your light shine before
others, that they may see your good deeds
and glorify your Father in heaven.
Matthew 5:16 (NIV)

Blessed are the peacemakers, for they
will be called children of God.
Matthew 5:9 (NIV)

Thank God for this gift too wonderful for words!
2 Corinthians 9:15 (NLT)

But the angel said to them, "Do not be afraid. I bring you good news that will cause great joy for all the people. Today in the town of David a Savior has been born to you; he is the Messiah, the Lord. This will be a sign to you: You will find a baby wrapped in cloths and lying in a manger."
Luke 2:10-12 (NIV)

This is how God showed his love among us: He sent his one and only Son into the world that we might live through him.
1 John 4:9 (NIV)

Peace I leave with you; my peace I give you. I do not give to you as the world gives. Do not let your hearts be troubled and do not be afraid.
John 14:27 (NIV)

May the God of hope fill you with all joy and peace as you trust in him, so that you may overflow with hope by the power of the Holy Spirit.
Romans 15:13 (NIV)

Therefore the Lord himself will give you a sign: The virgin will conceive and give birth to a son, and will call him Immanuel.
Isaiah 7:14 (NIV)

Every good and perfect gift is from above, coming down from the Father of the heavenly lights, who does not change like shifting shadows.
James 1:17 (NIV)

For God so loved the world that he gave his
one and only Son, that whoever believes in him
shall not perish but have eternal life.

John 3:16 (NIV)

In everything I did, I showed you that by this
kind of hard work we must help the weak,
remembering the words the Lord Jesus himself said:
"It is more blessed to give than to receive."

Acts 20:35 (NIV)

The Birth of Jesus

In those days Caesar Augustus issued a decree that a census should be taken of the entire Roman world. (This was the first census that took place while Quirinius was governor of Syria.) And everyone went to their own town to register.

So Joseph also went up from the town of Nazareth in Galilee to Judea, to Bethlehem the town of David, because he belonged to the house and line of David. He went there to register with Mary, who was pledged to be married to him and was expecting a child. While they were there, the time came for the baby to be born, and she gave birth to her firstborn, a son. She wrapped Him in cloths and placed Him in a manger, because there was no guest room available for them.

And there were shepherds living out in the fields nearby, keeping watch over their flocks at night. An angel of the Lord appeared to them, and the glory of the Lord shone around them, and they were terrified. But the angel said to them, "Do not be afraid. I bring you good news that will cause great joy for all the people. Today in the town of David a Savior has been born to you; he is the Messiah, the Lord. This will be a sign to you: you will find a baby wrapped in cloths and lying in a manger."

Suddenly a great company of the heavenly host appeared with the angel, praising God and saying, "Glory to God in the highest heaven, and on earth peace to those on whom his favor rests."

When the angels had left them and gone into heaven, the shepherds said to one another, "Let's go to Bethlehem and see this thing that has happened, which the Lord has told us about."

So they hurried off and found Mary and Joseph, and the baby, who was lying in the manger. When they had seen him, they spread the word concerning what had been told them about this child, and all who heard it were amazed at what the shepherds said to them. But Mary treasured up all these things and pondered them in her heart. The shepherds returned, glorifying and praising God for all the things they had heard and seen, which were just as they had been told.

Luke 2:1-20 (NIV)

New Year Prayer

Grant us, O Lord:
The hope to envision new dreams;
The strength to rise above our limitations,
our fears and whatever holds us down;
The courage to stand on our own,
to stretch our imagination
and to experience being fully human, fully alive;
The faith to live our lives in your image and likeness.
Guide us, O Lord, this new year,
every way, every day.
Amen.

Fr. Brian Cavanaugh, TOR

Endnotes

1. Exhaustive research failed to find the author of this story. Many stories circulate on the internet and in books for years, some for decades. Many different versions appear; some bear little resemblance to other versions. It is not unusual for no author to be given, or the attribution appears as "Author Unknown" or "Retold by…" While the majority of the works in this book were written by Barbara Russell Chesser, a few were adapted and or retold, including "My Perfect Christmas."

2. This story has been edited heavily (adapted) from a story. Permission was given by the nephew and sole heir of the deceased author.

3. This brief selection has been adapted. It has appeared in various forms on the internet and in numerous publications. No author has ever been found.

4. This brief selection has appeared in various forms on the internet and in numerous publications.

5. This brief selection has appeared in various forms on the internet and in numerous publications.

6. This selection has been adapted. It has appeared in various forms on the internet and in numerous publications.

7. Stanley Weintraub, *Silent Night: The Story of the World War I Christmas Truce* (New York: The Penguin Group, 2001), 44.

8. Jim Murphy, *Truce: The Day the Soldiers Stopped Fighting* (New York: Scholastic Press, 2009), 58.

9. Murphy, 59.

10. Murphy, 66.

11. David Mikkelson, "The Gold and Ivory Tablecloth." Last updated January 7, 2011. https://www.snopes.com/factcheck/the-gold-and-ivory-tablecloth/.

12. O. Henry, "The Gift of the Magi" in *The Gift of the Magi and Other Short Stories by O. Henry* (Digireads.com Publishing, 2018), 5-9.

13. Mother Teresa, *Where There Is Love, There Is God* (New York: Doubleday, 2010), 284.

14. Max Lucado, *God Came Near* (Nashville, TN: Thomas Nelson, 2004), 4.

ENDNOTES

15 Norman Vincent Peale, "How Wonderful That Christ Was Born," *Guideposts,* November 11, 2020. https://www.guideposts.org/inspiration/advent-day-9-how-wonderful-that-christ-was-born.

16 Calvin Coolidge, "A Christmas Message to the American People," *The Lincoln Star,* December 25, 1927.

17 Charles Dickens, *A Christmas Carol* (London, 1843; Project Gutenberg, 2004), http://www.gutenberg.org/ebooks/46.

18 Washington Irving, *Old Christmas: From the Sketch Book of Washington Irving* (London, 1886); Project Gutenberg, 2007), http://www.gutenberg.org/ebooks/20656.

19 Benjamin Franklin, *Poor Richard's Almanac: The Wit and Wisdom of Benjamin Franklin* (Seven Treasures Publications, 2008), 72.

20 Burton Hills, quoted in Jack Canfield, Mark Victor Hansen and Amy Newark, *The Gift of Christmas* (Cos Cob, CT: Chicken Soup for the Soul Publishing, LLC), 415.

21 Dale Evans, *A Happy Trails Christmas with Roy Rogers and Dale Evans* (Grand Rapids: Revell, 2012), 74-75.

22 Charles Haddon Spurgeon, "The First Christmas Carol," *New Park Street Pulpit,* vol. 4, December 20, 1857. https://www.spurgeon.org. resource-library.sermons.

23 John R. Rice, "The Shepherd's Christmas," *I Love Christmas* (Sword of the Lord, 1955), 26.

24 Pope Francis's midnight Mass, "Solemnity of the Nativity of the Lord," December 24, 2019. http://www.vatican.va/content/francesco/en/homilies/2019/documents/papa-francesco_20191224_omelia-natale.html.

25 Bob Hope, quoted in Lauren Chan and Leah Silverman, "The Most Inspiring Christmas Quotes of All Time," *Town and Country,* December 4, 2020. www.townandcountrymag.com/leisure/arts-and-culture/news/a2544/best-christmas-quotes.

26 Pope Francis, quoted in Julia Ludlam, "40+ Religious Christmas Quotes to Remind You of the Meaning of the Season," *Country Living,* December 6, 2020. https://www.countryliving.com/life/g28785956/religious-christmas-quotes.

27 Helen Steiner Rice, *Christmas Blessings,* (Grand Rapids: Revell, 1991).

28 Ronald Reagan, "A Message on the Observance of Christmas," December 11, 1986. www.reaganlibrary.gov/archives/speech/message-observance-christmas-1.

29 Helen Keller. *Out of the Dark: Essays, Lectures, and Addresses on Physical and Social Vision,* 1920.

30 Peter Marshall, *Let's Keep Christmas,* (New York: McGraw-Hill, 1953).

31 Pope John XXIII, *Days of Devotion: Daily Meditations from the Good Shepherd* (Viking Press, 1996).

32 Dr. Seuss (Theodor Seuss Geisel), *How the Grinch Stole Christmas* (New York: Random House Children's Books, 1957), 49.

33 Alexander Smith, "Christmas," 1863. *Quotidiana.* Ed. Patrick Madden, September 9, 2007.

34 George W. Truett, Presidential Address, 6th World Baptist Congress, Atlanta, 1939, http://bwa-baptist-heritage.org/wp-content/uploads/2016/07/George-W-Truiett.pdf.

35 Laura Ingalls Wilder, "As a Farm Woman Thinks," *Missouri Ruralist*, December 15, 1924. http://www.pioneergirl.com/ruralist_12_15_1924.jpg.

36 Winston Churchill, quoted in James Hume, *The Wit and Winston Churchill* (New York: Harper Perennial, 1995), 17.

37 Gloria Gaither, *He Started the Whole World Singing: A Treasury of Gaither Christmas Songs, Reflections, and Holiday Traditions* (New York: Time Warner Book Group, 2004), 171.

38 Rick Warren, "What Will You Find at Christmas," December 24, 1994.

39 Billy Graham, *The Cherished Works of Billy Graham* (Family Christian Press, 1988), 73.

40 David Jeremiah, Turning Points Magazine/Devotional 22, no. 12 (December 2020), 44.

41 Marjorie Holmes, *At Christmas the Heart Goes Home* (Doubleday, 1991).

42 Agnes M. Pharo, "What Is Christmas." This quote is widely attributed to Agnes M. Pharo and acknowledged by her family. www.agnespharo.com.

43 Amy Grant. "Christmas with Vince and Amy," interview by Alanna Nash, *Good Housekeeping*, November 9, 2011.

44 Corrie ten Boom, quoted in Julia Ludlam, "40+ Religious Christmas Quotes to Remind You of the Meaning of the Season," *Country Living*, December 6, 2020. https://www.countryliving.com/life/g28785956/religious-christmas-quotes.

45 Abigail Van Buren, "Dear Abby: A few years back," *Washington Post*, December 19, 2002. https://www.washingtonpost.com/archive/lifestyle/2002/12/19/dear-abby-a-few-years-back/599af755-5b06-4c8f-bcb6-5ce3bd21d2a2/.

About the Author

Barbara Russell Chesser, PhD, grew up hearing the deep rich chords of storytelling. Her interest in heartwarming stories and writing about these life experiences has resulted in numerous articles and books, including *Chicken Soup for the Golden Soul*, one of the bestselling books in the Chicken Soup series; it has appeared on all the major best-seller lists, sold more than one million copies, and is translated into nine languages.

Other books include *Remembering Mattie: A Pioneer Woman's Legacy of Grit, Gumption, and Grace*, an award-winning book about Barbara's grandmother; *21 Myths That Can Wreck Your Marriage*; and *Because You Care: Practical Ideas for Helping Those Who Grieve*. Co-authored books include a marriage and family college textbook and three other books. Barbara is the sole author of several other books and has also written for professional journals and popular magazines, including the *Journal of Religion and Health* and *Reader's Digest*.

After graduating at the top of her university class, Barbara earned her master's degree from Mills College (California) and her PhD from Texas Woman's University. She taught at the University of Nebraska, the University of Arkansas, the University of Nevada, and Chapman College (California), and she worked in the administration of Baylor University before becoming president of The Meyer Resource Group, a research and development company in a global enterprise serving affiliated companies in the United States and more than sixty countries throughout the world. Her work has taken her to

Greece, the Philippines, and the African countries of Nigeria, Tanzania, Swaziland, and Morocco. Barbara has received numerous awards for outstanding university teaching, research, and writing.

Barbara's home life centers on Del, a CPA and retired professor of accounting, Baylor University, Christi, their daughter (also a CPA), Michael, their son-in-law, and two grandchildren, Jackson and Ava.